CW00553654

NEWCASTLE UNITED

The 1968–69 Fairs Cup Story

NEWCASTLE UNITED

The 1968–69 Fairs Cup Story

40 Years on

JIM JEFFREY

First published in Great Britain in 2009 by
The Breedon Books Publishing Company Limited
Breedon House, 3 The Parker Centre,
Derby, DE21 4SZ.

© Jim Jeffrey, 2009

All Rights Reserved. No part of this publication may be reproduced, stored in a retrieval system, or transmitted in any form, or by any means, electronic, mechanical, photocopying, recording or otherwise without the prior permission in writing of the copyright holders, nor be otherwise circulated in any form or binding or cover other than in which it is published and without a similar condition being imposed on the subsequent publisher.

ISBN 978-1-85983-737-5

Printed and bound by TJ International, Padstow, Cornwall.

Contents

The Cast

Iam McFaul

David Craig

Frank Clark

Tommy Gibb

Ollie Burton

Bobby Moncur

Jim Scott

Bryan 'Pop' Robson

Wyn Davies

Preben Arentoft

Jackie Sinclair

Alan Foggon

John McNamee

John Craggs

David Elliott

Graham Winstanley

Geoff Allen

Keith Dyson

Arthur Horsfield

Jim Iley

Albert Bennett

Ron Guthrie

Dave Clarke

John Hope

Gordon Marshall

and

Joe Harvey

Acknowledgements

I am extremely grateful to the staff of the National Library of Scotland and The Mitchell Library for their assistance in ferrying vast amounts of newspapers to me. The local history section of Newcastle Central Library were also extraordinarily helpful. My own local library, the A.K. Bell in Perth, provided a very enjoyable working environment in the dark winter months. To Bobby Moncur and Jim Scott I owe special thanks for putting up with my many questions with good grace. Brian Johnston of Almondvale Programmes in Edinburgh was able to help me in sourcing United memorabilia from the 1960s, as was Peter Rundo from Gauldry, Fife. I had a remarkable amount of help from Nigel Mercer of Tasmania. His marvellous website of football cards of the 1960s and 1970s is a wonderful source of detail and entertainment.

Preface

Sitting here in 2009 it seems astonishing that the last time Newcastle United won a major honour was way back in 1969. As the memories of that glorious and surprising achievement become increasingly confined to the old BBC black-and-white highlights, occasional articles in the newspapers and yellowing memorabilia, it seems more important than ever to try and capture the essence of a bygone era and to cherish United's triumph.

A few years ago I interviewed Jim Scott in my capacity as Hibernian programme editor. We had a marvellous chat and the conversation at one point turned to how I'd been brought up in the north–east of England and that United's famous win in Budapest, indeed the whole Fairs Cup adventure, had been a touchstone for an entire football generation on Tyneside. At that point the memories flooded back and Jim opened up with recollections of not only the Final itself but of the wondrous, near mythical nights at St James' Park in that first European foray.

I wanted to know more and frankly I wanted to wallow in the nostalgia of the late 1960s. Fuelled by Jim's enthusiasm I sought out Bobby Moncur. Tracking down the former captain of United and Scotland was not easy and I was apprehensive about chatting to a sporting icon whom I had never met before. However, my fears were groundless. Bobby was a sheer delight and was quite happy to talk about Newcastle United's Inter-Cities Fairs Cup triumph at length. His lucid and fond recollections of his teammates, allied to his sheer enthusiasm, ensured that we shared a wonderful hour or so reliving the magic of the 1968–69 season.

Speaking to Bobby had been an indulgence as Hibs programme editor, but something was stirring in my mind. I felt that for all of the club histories of United out there, for all the hosts of magazine and newspaper articles, something was missing. Thus, I decided to try and piece together the memories of a quite specific and unexpected success of a famous club in a football–mad city some 40 years ago.

The city of Newcastle was reeling in the late 1960s; the world was an uncertain place but on dark evenings under the floodlights of St James' Park a magical world of escapism grew. Crackly radio commentaries, eagerly awaited morning newspapers and a clutch of returning fans told fascinating tales of the Magpies on the Continent. The suspense built until, remarkably, on a light, warm summer evening in June, United won the Inter-Cities Fairs Cup. I hope that in this book I have managed to capture some of the magic, some of the romance, of the late 1960s.

No matter what happens to Newcastle United in the future, the stunning achievement of that first-ever European adventure will remain a huge part of the club's tradition. It deserves to be cherished.

Introduction

Into Europe the Hard Way!

The tale of Newcastle United's 1969 Fairs Cup triumph is one of the great English football stories. Not only did the Magpies win a European competition at the very first attempt, but they also qualified for that competition not by winning a Cup or a Championship, but by virtue of finishing a very ordinary 10th place in the League! The fact that they have not won a major trophy since adds a little extra romance to their 1969 triumph.

The Inter-Cities Fairs Cup was, of course, no ordinary European competition. The European Cup was the preserve of League champions and the European Cup-Winners' Cup gained a touch of glamour by being solely open to national Cup winners, but the Fairs Cup was a much more complicated affair. The initial requirement was that clubs involved had to come from a city which held a trade fair, and the rule that proved most beneficial to Newcastle was that only one club per city was allowed entry.

It was this bizarre ruling that paved the way for Newcastle's magical adventure in the late 1960s.

The 1967–68 League campaign had been a poor, or at best average, one for United. They had lost more games than they had won; 14 defeats opposed to 13 wins. They had conceded 67 goals for only 54 scored, but they still slipped into Europe through an extraordinary set of circumstances.

In 1968 Manchester United won the European Cup, and also in 1968 Manchester City won the English Football League, thus, both Manchester sides qualified for Europe's premier competition. This, of course, had a knock-on effect down the top half of the League.

There were to be three English teams in the Fairs Cup and therefore the selection process should have been straightforward. Leeds United, as holders, were automatically guaranteed their place (which did not count as one of England's three allocated places) and after the champions and FA Cup winners (West Bromwich Albion) were removed from the equation the next-placed teams in the League were put forward for entry to the Inter-Cities tournament. This is where the fun began!

As explained above, City, as champions, went into the European Cup and by a strange twist of fate so too did second-placed Manchester United as European Cup holders. So, third-placed Liverpool were the first pick for the Fairs Cup. Fourth-placed Leeds were in too, of course. Fifth in the League were Everton, but as Liverpool were already in the tournament the blue half of Merseyside were unable to take part due to the 'one club per city' rule. This was no problem, the selectors simply moved on to the sixth-placed team, Chelsea. The Stamford Bridge club gratefully accepted the opportunity. There then remained just one place to fill.

Standing at seventh were Tottenham, but they were ruled out because they, like Chelsea, were a London-based club. By now the selection process was down to eighth position and it stumbled upon the FA Cup holders, who in this instance were West Bromwich Albion. The men from the Hawthorns, in winning the FA Cup, had secured the only spot available for an English club in the European Cup-Winners' Cup. Extraordinarily, this meant that the search for the final English participant in the Fairs Cup had to continue and so the authorities, late in the day, decided to extend the English League's allocation in the competition.

Now things were getting surreal. The team that had finished the campaign in ninth place was the next club invited into the glamorous European competition, and they too remarkably proved unable to take up the offer as they were capital-based Arsenal.

1967–68
Division One

	P	W	D	L	F	A	Pts
Manchester C.	42	26	6	10	86	43	58
Manchester U.	42	24	8	10	89	55	56
Liverpool	42	22	11	9	71	40	55
Leeds U.	42	22	9	11	71	41	53
Everton	42	23	6	13	67	40	52
Chelsea	42	18	12	12	62	68	48
Tottenham H.	42	19	9	14	70	59	47
W.B.A.	42	17	12	13	75	62	46
Arsenal	42	17	10	15	60	56	44
Newcastle U	**42**	**13**	**15**	**14**	**54**	**67**	**41**
Nottingham F.	42	14	11	17	52	64	39
West Ham U.	42	14	10	18	73	69	38
Leicester C.	42	13	12	17	64	69	38
Burnley	42	14	10	18	64	71	38
Sunderland	42	13	11	18	51	61	37
Southampton	42	13	11	18	66	83	37
Wolverhampton W.	42	14	8	20	66	75	36
Stoke C.	42	14	7	21	50	73	35
Sheffield W.	42	11	12	19	51	63	34
Coventry C.	42	9	15	18	51	71	33
Sheffield U.	42	11	10	21	49	70	32
Fulham	42	10	7	25	56	98	27

(see table in appendix for home and away breakdown)

So, this bizarre series of events is the reason why the invitation into Europe finally landed at the door of 10th-placed Newcastle United. For the first time ever United were into Europe, but who could have imagined a 10th-place finish in the League meriting European qualification? When the previous season had stuttered towards its conclusion it was only in the very final weeks that Novocastrians began to think that there could be a bizarrely happy outcome to the end of a mediocre campaign. For much of the season thoughts of excursions to play in European competition had been far removed from any Geordie minds.

That such an unlikely route into Europe should end in glory makes the story of the 1968–69 Fairs Cup triumph all the more compelling. Forty years on it is still a story worth retelling.

When Newcastle United entered European competition they had something to live up to. English clubs had an undoubtedly sound heritage in European football. Since Tottenham Hotspur had won the European Cup-Winners' Cup in 1963, and thus became the first British team to win in Europe, there had been strong offensives to bring back European silverware.

The English story in the Fairs Cup was particularly impressive. Since a London representative XI had contested the first Final in 1955 there had been consistent English challenges. In 1960 and 1961 Birmingham City had reached the Finals only to fall at that last prestigious hurdle. Manchester United were downed by Ferencváros in the 1965 semi-finals and in 1966 England saw both Leeds and Chelsea reach the last four, only for both to lose to Spanish opposition. In 1967 Leeds United had lost to Dinamo Zagreb in the Final, but one year later, and in the year before Newcastle participated, Leeds won the trophy by beating Ferencváros.

The competition, when viewed today, seems as dated in concept as it was in format. It came into being in April 1955 and initially tapped into the

European fondness for holding prestige trade fairs. The early competition insisted that only cities that held renowned international trade fairs could compete, and it was cities rather than clubs that took part – thus, the early contestants were Barcelona, Basle, Birmingham, Copenhagen, Frankfurt, Lausanne, Leipzig, London, Milan and Zagreb. The London team featured players from Arsenal, Tottenham, Chelsea, West Ham, Fulham, Brentford, Orient, Crystal Palace, Millwall and QPR. The tournament made what Brian Glanville, a leading football writer, beautifully called 'a creaking start'. That first Cup ran astonishingly from 1955 to 1958, and when the Final eventually limped into view it was a two-legged showdown between London and Barcelona. At Stamford Bridge, home of Chelsea, London were held 2–2 by the Catalans, and in Barcelona the Spaniards made good use of that advantage by winning heavily 6–2. It is worth noting that the authorities in Barcelona used only Barca players and did not call upon the likes of Espanyol for assistance.

The 1958–59 tournament saw cities represented by clubs from the trade fair centres rather than consciously composite sides. This time Birmingham City reached the Final but again Barcelona thwarted British ambitions. In England's second city they drew 0–0 as a prelude to administering a 4–1 humbling at Camp Nou. Birmingham repeated their march to the Final in 1961 but this time lost out to Roma; again after a draw in England. Eventually the cunning Spaniards of Barcelona were ousted by a British side but only after a brawl with Hibernian in Edinburgh, and brawling would soon become an entertaining side–show that peppered the history of the Fairs Cup.

While it is beyond the scope of this book it is nevertheless interesting to note that from Leeds and Newcastle winning the 1968 and 1969 Fairs Cups there was a five-year run when the trophy never left England's shores.

It was not just in the Fairs Cup that English ambitions were shining brightly. In 1965 West Ham United had won the European Cup-Winners' Cup (just two years after Spurs' memorable breakthrough success) and Liverpool had later contested the 1966 Final. And, of course, the icing on the English cake had come in 1968 when Manchester United won the biggest club competition of all – the European Cup.

So, while Newcastle were complete novices in the European competition stakes they could at least call upon a recent run of English triumphs for inspiration. Indeed, they entered the competition at a time when English clubs were about to leave an indelible mark on Europe and earn seriously impressive reputations. Few on the Continent may have heard of Newcastle United but by dint of being an English club side they carried a little bit of threat despite their novice status!

Nineteen sixty-eight was a year of considerable change. On the world stage America was embroiled in what would prove a costly war in Vietnam, both economically and socially. In April Martin Luther King was assassinated and a few weeks later the world held its breath when the same fate befell a young Robert Kennedy. By the time the year had ended the Soviet Union and her allies had invaded Czechoslovakia and 'the Troubles' in Northern Ireland had erupted.

Compared to such cataclysmic international events life in Newcastle went on at a fairly sedate pace in 1968. It was not without excitement or change, but things were of a more serene nature than on the world stage. The city welcomed the King of Norway, Olav the fifth, to open the new civic centre, a building that had cost an almost unprecedented £5 million to complete. In November 1968 the latest British pop sensation The Who were in town at Newcastle City Hall, and comic script writers Dick Clement and Ian La Frenais were turning their thoughts to a new series of *The Likely Lads* for BBC television.

It is hardly surprising, therefore, that few people took much notice of Newcastle United making a belated entry into what was traditionally a rather bloated European football competition. The near farcical nature of their inclusion in the Fairs Cup had hardly merited a fanfare of trumpets to herald the arrival of the Magpies on the European stage. When the draw was finally made United were paired with Dutch side Feyenoord of Rotterdam. The tie was due to see the first leg played on Tyneside in mid-September, and by that time (although the season only started on 10 August) United would have no fewer than nine matches under their belt. English football, long renowned for its fixture congestion and gruelling campaigns, was not disposed to making life easy for its European representatives or, indeed, its national side!

The season started promisingly for Newcastle. West Ham United, still boasting their World Cup-winning trio of Hurst, Peters and Moore, rolled into St James' Park on the opening day to thrill a crowd of over 36,000. A 1–1 draw ensued and four days later that was also the outcome of United's second League match, this time at a more sparsely populated Hillsborough against Sheffield Wednesday.

On 17 August United tasted their first defeat of the campaign when they slipped to a 1–0 reversal at Burnley's tight Turf Moor ground, but the second midweek game of the season, at home to Chelsea, saw United win a five-goal thriller with almost 40,000 squeezing into St James'. Such a crowd would pale into insignificance as a remarkable season unfolded.

The games were coming thick and fast with no midweek respites, and the third Saturday of the season saw United draw 0–0 at home to Everton with just under 39,000 paying for the pleasure. There was time for a 1–1 draw at Nottingham Forest before the month of August ended with a seventh League fixture. This time the opponents were fierce local rivals Sunderland, and almost bang on 50,000 were inside Roker Park to witness a thrilling 1–1 draw. Neither side had been 'setting the heather on fire', but that mattered little with local pride at stake. The match was all-ticket and sold out well in advance, and the capacity crowd saw Bryan 'Pop' Robson give the Magpies a first-half lead, but United failed to capitalise on their domination of the opening 45 minutes and paid the price in the second half when Sunderland equalised through Colin Suggett. After that both sides had chances to win the game but there was no further scoring. United had dominated three quarters of the match with their 'power play', but unfortunately they lacked the necessary guile to secure a victory.

Bryan 'Pop' Robson.

Thus, from the seven opening games of the League campaign United had won one, lost one and rather surprisingly drawn five. The club were still a big draw at the gate for all their mid-table anonymity, however, and 239,907 had been eager enough to pay at the turnstiles to watch the Magpies start their campaign.

Feyenoord were now on the horizon but still there was time to squeeze in another couple of matches. Lowly Southport were beaten in a League Cup tie 2–0 in Merseyside and then Coventry City inflicted United's second defeat of the campaign when they edged home 2–1 at Highfield Road.

The 11th day of September dawned with United having made steady but unspectacular progress in the new season.

Feyenoord

A Dutch Treat as United Step Into Europe

FIRST ROUND, FIRST LEG

11 September 1968

Newcastle United 4 **Feyenoord 0**

Scott 6, Robson 26, Gibb 42, Davies 72

Newcastle: McFaul, Craig, Clark, Gibb, McNamee, Burton, Scott, Robson, Davies, Elliott, Allen.

Subs: Marshall, Sinclair, Iley.

Feyenoord: Graafland, van der Heide, Israel, Laseroms, Veldhoen, Boskamp, Jansen, Wery, Kindvall, van Hanegem, Moulijn.

Sub: Geels.

Attendance: 46,348

Referee: Hans Carlsson (Sweden)

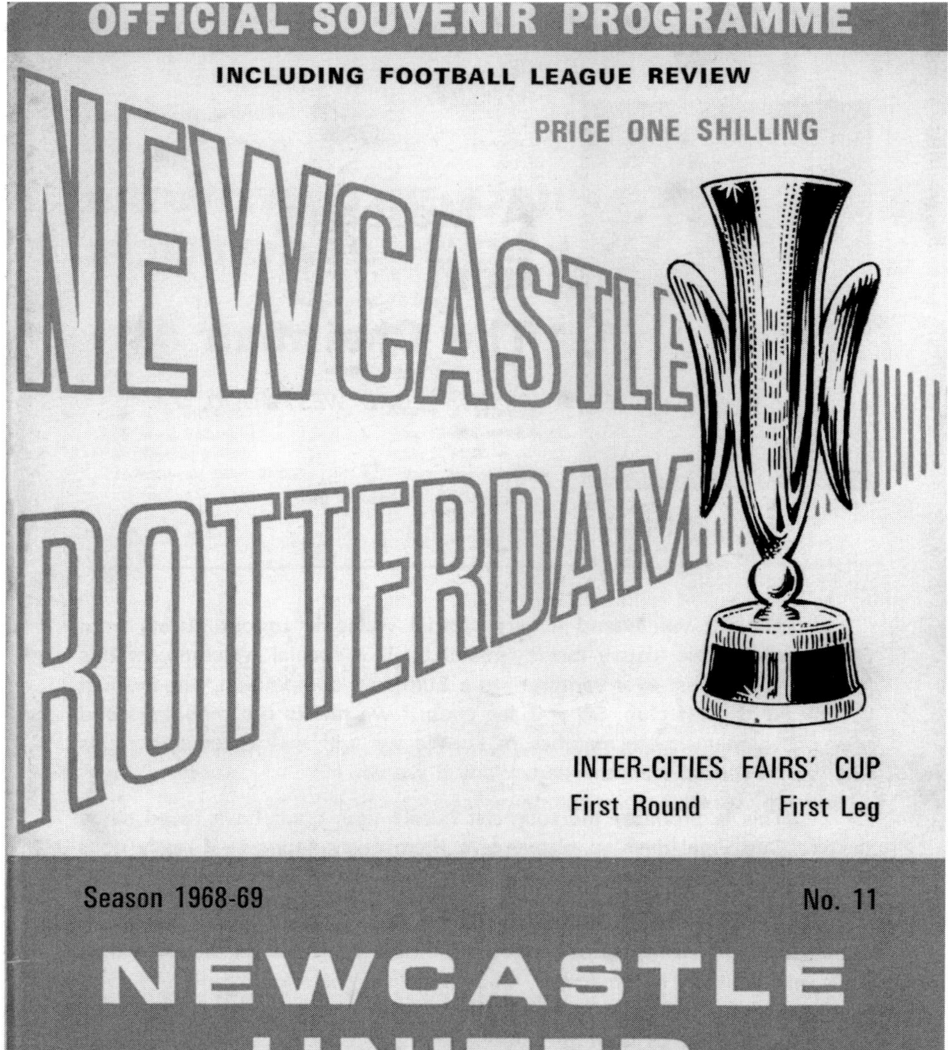
OFFICIAL SOUVENIR PROGRAMME
INCLUDING FOOTBALL LEAGUE REVIEW
PRICE ONE SHILLING
NEWCASTLE
ROTTERDAM
INTER-CITIES FAIRS' CUP
First Round First Leg
Season 1968-69
No. 11
NEWCASTLE UNITED
ST. JAMES' PARK - NEWCASTLE UPON TYNE
VERSUS
FEYENOORD
Wednesday, 11th September, 1968
Kick-off 7-30 p.m.

Nineteen sixty-eight was in some ways a 'crossroads' year. There was a section of society looking back on the huge changes since 1945 and the end of World War Two, and another section of society was looking forward to a new political order. Thus a series of protests and demonstrations punctuated what was an uncertain period. This was reflected in the great literary works of the day. While John le Carré captured the post-war political tension in his *Small Town in Germany*, Arthur C. Clarke took an entirely different approach and his *2001: A Space Odyssey* took science fiction to a new level in an era increasingly dominated by man's fascination with space and landing on the moon.

Newcastle United's ambitions were a little more down to earth, though. Quite simply the club just wanted to give a good account of themselves in European competition. But they could have hoped for easier opposition in their first-ever European tie. In being paired with Feyenoord of Rotterdam they were facing not just one of Holland's biggest clubs but also a side with a strong European reputation. The men from Rotterdam were no slouches on the domestic front and were indeed destined to land both the Dutch League and Cup in 1969, and remarkably just over a year later they would stand proudly as champions of Europe.

By and large Feyenoord had enjoyed the 1960s. They had won the Dutch title in both 1960 and 1961, and in 1963 they had reached the semi-finals of the European Cup. In the latter tournament it was only coming up against the mighty Portuguese champions Benfica that halted their progress. When they won the domestic title again in 1965 it was their third League Championship in just six seasons, but they got a lesson when they subsequently took their place in the European Cup. Paired with the legendary Real Madrid they were soundly thrashed 5–0 in Spain.

Thus Feyenoord came into the Newcastle match with an impressive pedigree. But they were wary of English opposition as their only home defeat in the European Cup had been to the Spurs double-winning side of 1961. However, the Feyenoord squad contained a cast of internationally qualified players. Arguably their best player was goalkeeper Eddy Pieters Graafland, who at 35 years old was probably at his very peak. He had been with fierce rivals Ajax Amsterdam from 1952 to 1958 and then made the unconventional switch to Rotterdam, where he racked up almost 400 appearances. United's task was to not only penetrate a well drilled defence, but also to beat a goalkeeper of international repute.

As if to prove their credentials, Feyenoord started the 1968–69 season in powerful fashion. On the opening day of their League campaign they had won 3–2 at Maastrict and then in quick succession they turned over DWS Amsterdam (a 3–0 home win which United boss Joe Harvey spied on), PSV Eindhoven and AZ Alkmaar, scoring eight goals and conceding none in the process. Just seven days before Feyenoord played in Newcastle, four of their players had helped Holland beat Luxembourg 2–0 in Rotterdam in a World Cup qualifier. It was notable that Wim Jansen and Willem van Hanegem, two Feyenoord stalwarts, had netted the Dutch goals.

The Rotterdam internationals

Eddy Pieters Graafland	47 Netherlands caps
Piet Romeijn	4 Netherlands caps
Cor Veldhoen	26 Netherlands caps
Spasoje Samardzić	26 Yugoslavia caps
Henk Wery	10 Netherlands caps
Willem van Hanegem	2 Netherlands caps
Coen Moulijn	35 Netherlands caps
Ove Kindvall	10 Sweden caps
Wim Jansen	7 Netherlands caps
Marinus Israel	13 Netherlands caps

Jim Scott, scorer of Newcastle's first European goal after just six minutes. Jim also played 12 times for Hibs in Europe.

Based in the imposing De Kuip Stadium, Feyenoord would present formidable opponents for European novices, and especially for a club that had managed a mere 10th-place finish in their League competition. The form book rather suggested that Rotterdam's finest were in far better shape than the pride of the Tyne. Yet, while the evening on Tyneside proved decidedly one-sided, it was one-sided in favour of Newcastle. United romped to a staggering 4–0 victory that all but reduced the second leg to a mere formality.

Newcastle may have been newcomers to European football, but a few of their stars were far from being apprentices. Most notably the two Scottish wingers – Jim Scott and Jackie Sinclair – were veterans of European football with numerous appearances and goals to their names

Bryan 'Pop' Robson narrowly misses for Newcastle.

TOP OF THE CHARTS

Hey Jude
The Beatles
I've Gotta Get a Message to You
The Bee Gees
Do It Again
Beach Boys
I Say a Little Prayer
Aretha Franklin
Hold Me Tight
Johnny Nash
This Guy's In Love With You
Herb Alpert
Those Were the Days
Mary Hopkin
Help Yourself
Tom Jones
High In the Sky
Amen Corner
On The Road Again
Canned Heat

from their spells at Hibs and Dunfermline respectively.

United made a dream start to the match. Only six minutes had elapsed when Geoff Allen swung over a cross that picked out Bryan 'Pop' Robson, and his headed knock-down was drilled home by Jim Scott. Thus, the former Hibernian man had the honour of being Newcastle's first-ever European marksman.

The goal really boosted Newcastle and removed any nerves from their play. Allen, who was in inspirational form, and arguably gave his finest showing in a Newcastle jersey that night, smacked a shot off the crossbar, and when Wyn Davies did likewise Robson was on hand to send a diving header home from the rebound in the 26th minute. The men from Rotterdam were stunned, and even more so when they conceded a third before the break. Tommy Gibb, who had only recently joined Newcastle from Partick Thistle, found space to get in a powerful shot which was deflected on its way beyond Graafland in the Feyenoord goal.

In the second half the St James' Park floodlights came into their own. Lights at St James' had first lit up the Tyneside night sky in February 1953 when Celtic were the guests, and a few years later they were dramatically improved, to the extent that the Football League hosted League international matches on the banks of the Tyne.

Almost inevitably United could not repeat such heroics in the second half, but they did tease. Then Feyenoord's first-team coach Ben Peeters tried

Feyenoord's De Kuip Stadium

desperately to salvage something from the tie (Guus Brox, who was shown in the match programme, was actually general manager, a position distinct from first-team coach) but his plans backfired when he replaced Willem van Hanegem with Geels in the 67th minute. Feyenoord were at sixes and sevens as they reorganised following the substitution, and almost immediately Newcastle seized on the Rotterdam club's indecision and in the 72th minute Davies added goal number four, heading home from a Scott cross.

It was a marvellous win for Newcastle and one which left them ideally prepared for the short trip over the North Sea to Rotterdam.

First round, second leg

17 September 1968

Feyenoord 2 **Newcastle United 0**

Kindvall 28, van der Heide 54

(Newcastle won 4–2 on aggregate)

Newcastle: McFaul, Craig, Clark, Gibb, McNamee, Burton, Scott, Robson, Davies, Elliott, Allen.
Subs: Iley, Marshall, Sinclair.
Feyenoord: Graafland, Romeijn, Israel, Laseroms, Veldhoen, Boskamp, Jansen, Wery, Kindvall, van Hanegem, Moulijn.
Sub: van der Heide.

Attendance: 45,000
Referee: Fritz (West Germany)

The return leg in Holland was a game in which Feyenoord proved their reputation for quality was not an illusion. But while the mighty Dutch giants would win the European Cup by defeating Celtic in Milan in 1970, in 1968 against Newcastle United they found a four-goal deficit too much to overcome, despite showing their class.

Rotterdam is an impressive footballing city, indeed it has much in common with Newcastle-upon-Tyne. Very much an industrial port, it has a long history of shipbuilding, brewing and the energy industry. Rotterdam is substantially larger than Newcastle, however, and it was petroleum rather than coal that fuelled trade here, but swap the Maas-Rhine delta for the Tyne and the symmetry is clear. Arguably the major port in Europe, the city needed its escapism and was in love with its football team which vied with Amsterdam's Ajax for supremacy in The Netherlands.

Home for Feyenoord was the imposing De Kuip Stadium, which had recently been refurbished at a cost of around £4 million and could house 62,000 fans. The club name Feyenoord was taken from the district in which the De Kuip was sited, and although the official name of the stadium was actually the Feyenoord Stadium, given the stadium's appearance it was nicknamed De Kuip, which translates from Dutch to

English as 'The Tub'. It had been specifically designed under the instructions of the club president Leen van Zandvliet to keep all of the available noise in to create a cauldron-like atmosphere, which explains the stadium's shape. The vociferous and fiercely supportive Feyenoord fans were arrayed around the pitch in two tiers and more than half of them were (unusually from a British perspective) seated.

The city of Rotterdam had one other great allure…it was there in 1963 that Tottenham Hotspur had become the very first British side to win a European competition, and that Cup-Winners' Cup Final had gone so well (between Spurs and Atletico Madrid) that the 1968 Final had been held there too.

Such was the novelty of playing away in Europe that the Newcastle United supporters' club had to learn quickly how to organise a trip to foreign shores. The highly-motivated development association, with the assistance of two commercial firms (Callers Pegasus Travel and Riviera Holidays), arranged charter flights for the princely sum of almost £20, which gave United fans transfers to and from the airport but also an overnight stay and an educational sightseeing tour. Actually, the trip cost £15 and 15 shillings, and if fans stretched to £19 and 10 shillings a match ticket would be included. Over 2,000 United fans decided this was money well spent and headed off on a trip that was greatly assisted by the input of the enthusiastic *Newcastle Chronicle*.

The first big difference the Geordie visitors noticed inside the stadium was the noise. Of course, Tynesiders were used to football noise but normally the volume was created by vocal roars. In Rotterdam it was the claxons, fireworks and whistles that created the background wall of sound. The stadium's unique design simply enhanced the impressive acoustics.

Feyenoord, in the their traditional red-and-white halved tops, sprung a major change in the run-up to this game. Out went first-team coach Ben Peeters and in came a man who would stride across European football – Ernst

Feyenoord's Coen Moulijn.

Happel. The hosts started the match at a cracking pace and were buzzing around Iam McFaul's goal in no time. A couple of excellent saves blunted the Rotterdam passion, but in the 28th minute a free-kick by the brilliant Ove Kindvall zipped low beyond McFaul as the hosts reduced the Dutch arrears. For the excited and confident United fans who had made the journey, the sight of their favourites being so easily pulled apart was more than a little disconcerting.

Newcastle weathered the storm, however, with man-mountain John McNamee and the experienced Ollie Burton in determined mood at the heart of the Geordies' defence. In the 54th minute Feyenoord scored the second goal that their pressure merited, when substitute Frans van der Heide picked up a loose ball and scored from an impossibly tight angle.

John McNamee...a Scottish 'rock'.

United hung on as the men from Rotterdam's docklands threw the proverbial kitchen sink at them, and although there were a few narrow escapes, it is fair to say that the four-goal cushion established at St James' Park was never under undue threat.

After the match the Dutch club showed a touch of class and sense of occasion by presenting each member of the United side with a clock as a souvenir. Feyenoord were then free to concentrate on winning their national double of League Championship and Dutch Cup, which they duly did. A year on they won the European Cup, but they would always remember the humbling handed out by those upstarts from Newcastle.

Rotterdam Heroes

WIM JANSEN

Born: Rotterdam, 28 October 1946.
Career as a player: Feyenoord (1965–80), Washington Diplomats (1980), Ajax Amsterdam (1980–82), Washington Diplomats (1982).
Career as a manager: Lokeren (1987–88), Feyenoord (1990–93), Hiroshima (1994–97), Celtic (1997–98), Urawa Red Diamonds (2000–03).

Wim Jansen.

Midfielder Wim Jansen was essentially the local boy made good. He played in over 400 matches for the Rotterdam club, winning four titles and famously the European Cup in 1970. He was capped 65 times at international level and represented Holland in both the 1974 and 1978 World Cup Finals (which were lost to West Germany and Argentina in the hosts' countries). Although he spent a short time at the great rivals of Feyenoord – Ajax of Amsterdam – his name was more readily linked to his first club.

Wim's coaching career was also dominated by spells with Feyenoord. He cut his teeth as a youth coach and assistant manager before striking out on his own in Belgium and then returning to manage Feyenoord for three years. Perhaps his most interesting spell as a manager came in Britain when he bossed Celtic for a solitary season, starting in the summer of 1997, and won the Championship…a win which prevented Rangers from snatching a record-breaking 10th consecutive title. He was also the man who signed arguably Celtic's most successful post-war player – Henrik Larsson. In 2005, after sojourns in the Middle East and Far East, Wim was appointed technical advisor to his beloved Feyenoord.

OVE KINDVALL

Born: Norrköping, 16 May 1943.

Career as a player: Norrköping (1962–66), Feyenoord (1966–71), Norrköping (1971–75), IFK Gothenburg (1975–77).

Career after football: Chairman of IFK Gothenburg in the 1979–80 season.

Ove Kindvall.

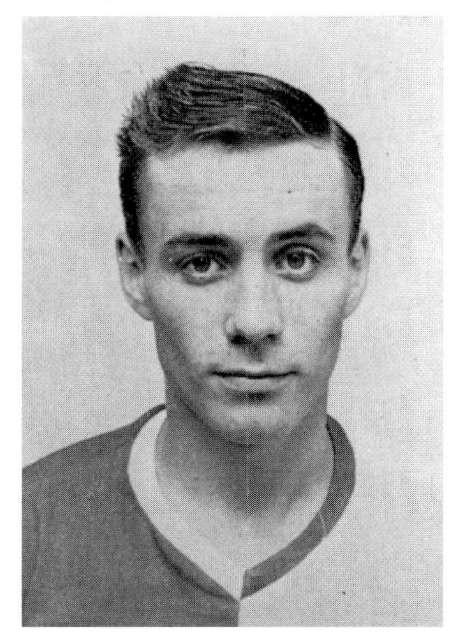

Like that other great Swedish centre-forward, Gunnar Nordahl, Ove started out with Norrköping. A prolific striker for Sweden, he grabbed 16 goals in 43 internationals and was Swedish Footballer of the

Year in 1966. That award was the springboard for his move to Holland and Kindvall established himself as a Feyenoord legend over six wonderful years. He amassed a staggering 129 goals in only 144 League games and was the top scorer in the Dutch League on three occasions. In the 1967–68 season he bagged 28 goals, and he scored two more than that in the following season. But perhaps the pinnacle of his time in Rotterdam came in 1970 when he scored the extra-time winner in the European Cup Final against Celtic. Quick, fearless and a wonderful header of the ball, Kindvall at his peak was a class act.

EDDY PIETERS GRAAFLAND

Born: Amsterdam, 5 January 1934.

Career as a player: Ajax Amsterdam (1952–58), Feyenoord (1958–70).

Career after football: Youth coach at Feyenoord (1979–81).

Eddy Pieters Graafland.

One of the great goalkeepers of his era, Graafland played over 150 games for Ajax before moving to Rotterdam. He proved his credentials at Feyenoord, where he made over 350 outings. His international career spanned 10 years and brought 47 appearances. When Feyenoord won the 1970 European Cup Final against Celtic, Graafland, Israel, Jansen, van Hanegem, Wery, Kindvall and Moulijn were survivors from the defeat to Newcastle, but the man in charge by that stage was Ernst Happel.

First Round Results in Full

Aris (Salonika) v. Hibernians (Malta)	1–0	6–0	7–0
Athletic Bilbao v. Liverpool	2–1	1–2	3–3x aet
Atletico Madrid v. KSV Waregem	2–1	0–1	2–2*
Beerschot VAV v. DWS (Amsterdam)	1–1	1–2	2–3
Bologna v. FC Basle	4–1	2–1	6–2
Chelsea v. Morton	5–0	4–3	9–3
Daring CB v. Panathinaikos	2–1	0–2	2–3
DOS (Utrecht) v. Dundalk	1–1	1–2	2–3 aet
FC Hansa Rostock v. OGC Nice	3–0	1–2	4–2
FC Metz v. Hamburger SV	1–4	2–3	3–7
FC Slavia (Sofia) v. Aberdeen	0–0	0–2	0–2
FC Trakia (Plovdiv) v. Real Zaragoza	3–1	0–2	3–3*
FK Skeid v. AIK (Stockholm)	1–1	1–2	2–3
Göztepe v. Olympique Marseille	2–0	0–2	2–2x aet
Hannover 96 v. B1909 (Odense)	3–2	1–0	4–2
Lausanne-Sports v. Juventus	0–2	0–2	0–4
Legia Warsaw v. TSV 1860 Munich	6–0	3–2	9–2
Leixoes SC v. FC Arges (Pitesti)	1–1	0–0	1–1*
Newcastle United v. Feyenoord	4–0	0–2	4–2
NK Dinamo (Zagreb) v. AC Fiorentina	1–1	1–2	2–3
NK Olimpija (Ljubljana) v. Hibernian	0–3	1–2	1–5
O. Lyonnais v. Académica Coimbra	1–0	0–1	1–1x aet
Rangers v. FK Vojvodina (Novi Sad)	2–0	0–1	2–1
Rapid Bucharest v. OFK Belgrade	3–1	1–6	4–7 aet
Sporting CP (Lisbon) v. Valencia	4–0	1–4	5–4
SSC Napoli v. Grasshopper-Club Zürich	3–1	0–1	3–2
Standard CL (Liege) v. Leeds United	0–0	2–3	2–3

Vitória Setúbal *v.* Linfield	3–0	3–1	6–1
Wacker Innsbruck *v.* Eintracht Frankfurt	2–2	0–3	2–5
Wiener Sport-Club *v.* Slavia Prague	1–0	0–5	1–5

x Athletic Bilbao, Olympique Lyonnais and Göztepe progressed on a coin toss

Lokomotive Leipzig walkover, KB (Copenhagen) withdrew

Újpest Dozsa walkover, US Luxembourg withdrew

* Indicates a win on the away goals rule

Sporting Lisbon

A Sporting Chance

SECOND ROUND, FIRST LEG

30 October 1968

Sporting Lisbon 1 | **Newcastle United 1**

Morais 89 | *Scott 31*

Sporting: Damas, Celestino, Conceiçáo, Goncalves, Armando, Carlos, Chico, Ernesto, Lourenco, Morais, Pedras.

Sub: Marinho.

Newcastle United: McFaul, Craig, Clark, Gibb, Winstanley, Burton, Scott, Robson, Davies, Moncur, Foggon.

Subs: Dyson, Clarke, Elliott.

Attendance; 9,000

Referee: J. Wetter

Season 1968-69

No. 22

NEWCASTLE UNITED

ST. JAMES' PARK - NEWCASTLE UPON TYNE

VERSUS

SPORTING CLUB de PORTUGAL

Wednesday, 20th November, 1968

Kick-off 7-30 p.m.

The José Alvalade Stadium

Having won the European Cup-Winners' Cup in 1964 and the Portuguese League in 1966, there was no doubting the impressive credentials of Sporting Lisbon (or to give them their seldom-used correct name, Sporting Club de Portugal). The men from Lisbon had a proud heritage to call upon, indeed the first-ever European Cup game had seen Sporting tackle Partizan Belgrade in Lisbon and one of their forwards – Joao Baptista Martins – had netted the first-ever European goal in a 3–3 draw.

Home for the Lisbon side was the José Alvalade Stadium, which while older than the De Kuip in Rotterdam had nevertheless had something of a recent face-lift and even included a 40 bedroom hotel in its build. The José Alvalade Stadium was named after its founder from 1906 and had been formally opened on 1 July 1956. A huge stadium, it lay on the roadside not far from Lisbon Airport and was testimony to the wealthy Lisbon family that gifted their land to get 'The Lions' up and running.

How Newcastle's fans and officials must have envied the state of the Continental stadiums. Having missed out on hosting the 1966 World Cup matches that came to the North East (instead Sunderland and

Middlesbrough were given the honour of hosting games), it was clear that St James' Park would need some form of upgrade in the future.

Lisbon, rather like Rotterdam, had the allure of being a major port with a significant footprint in history. Again there was a shipbuilding connection with Tyneside, and it was clear to those Newcastle fans who took the chance to tour the city before the game that they were in a major national capital with a great heritage. And whereas Rotterdam city centre had been largely rebuilt after suffering huge damage in World War Two, Portugal, as a neutral state, had avoided such devastation and Lisbon remained the glorious capital it had been for hundreds of years.

The men from Lisbon had reached this stage of the competition thanks largely to a tremendous 4–0 home win over Spanish giants Valencia. Yet that was not enticement enough to fill the stadium for the match against United; indeed, on a night of torrential rain the local populace clearly found other forms of entertainment and only 9,000 passed through the turnstiles...this was perhaps evidence of the huge drawback of only having one part of the ground covered. United, of course, had no household names and no European heritage to call upon, so the lack of local interest on a filthy evening was understandable. Even those who had studied Newcastle from afar would have been scurrying for information on an unfamiliar name who made his European debut in Lisbon. Graham Winstanley was hardly well-known in England, let alone Portugal. With teenager Alan Foggon also in the starting XI it was a far from familiar United team that ran out for action.

Newcastle had played seven League matches and one League Cup tie since easing through in Rotterdam. Crushed in the League Cup by Southampton 4–1 in Hampshire, there had been better fortune in the League with wins against Nottingham Forest, Ipswich Town and QPR, with United scoring four goals in the first two games which were away

The 1968–69 Sporting Lisbon team, some of whom played against Newcastle in the Fairs Cup. Back row (left to right): Conceiçáo, Barao, Pedro Gomes, Alexandre Batista, Manhica, Carvalho. Front row: Mateus, Lourenco, Vitor Goncalves, Figueiredo, Peres.

matches. But against the 'big boys' of Manchester United, Leeds and Liverpool, Newcastle had shown up badly and lost each and every time.

Immediately prior to the Sporting match Newcastle had travelled to Liverpool and lost 2–1, a defeat which ended a run of three consecutive victories. It seemed as though the only hope for European progression was that Sporting would not be as powerful as the likes of Leeds or Liverpool. Bobby Moncur was back in the United squad after he missed the early season through injury and was patched up after breaking his nose on Merseyside.

From the off Lisbon were keen to prove that their demolition of Valenica was no fluke. Sensing that Newcastle were inexperienced at this level, and notoriously vulnerable away from the cauldron of St James' Park, Lisbon placed Newcastle under intense early pressure and Celestino, the ever-adventurous full-back, smacked an early effort off the United crossbar.

Yet United stunned their hosts by scoring the opening goal after 31 minutes. Frank Clark launched a long free-kick into the Lisbon penalty area, and when Robson controlled the ball he retained enough composure to set-up Jim Scott for a wonderful goal.

TOP OF THE CHARTS

Bad Moon Rising
Credence Clearwater Revival
I'll Never Fall In Love Again
Bobby Gentry
Je T'aime – Moi Non Plus
Jane Birkin and Serge Gainsbourg
A Boy Named Sue
Johnny Cash
Don't Forget To Remember
The Bee Gees
Good Morning Starshine
Oliver
Throw Down A Line
Cliff and Hank
It's Getting Better
Mama Cass
Lay Lady Lay
Bob Dylan
In The Year 2525
Zager and Evans

The incessant rain had not relented by a fraction and by half-time both sides were soaked. Lisbon, at home and with access to all their resources, wisely changed from their sodden traditional green-and-white hoops into a dry kit that showed green-and-white halves. It was more than a little bit like being up against Feyenoord again!

Unfortunately, a famous away victory was snatched from United's grasp in the final seconds. There was less than a minute to go when Morais escaped his marker to fire in a shot that hit the bar but fortunately struck the arm of McFaul before dropping over the line. It was a lifeline for Lisbon and one which made their forthcoming trip to England just that little bit more encouraging. For United, however, this was a wonderful display and the tie was set up perfectly for a raucous Tyneside night.

The Sporting coach Fernando Caiado was downcast after the game. Working on a short-term contract, he was aware that his job was becoming increasingly threatened. Bemoaning that he did not have the stability of a longer contract, he was also aware that Sporting's notoriously fickle ownership were not shy in dismissing coaches they deemed to have failed. Otto Gloria, who had steered Portugal to third place in the 1966 World Cup Finals, had been dismissed after an unproductive season, and Caiado was aware that his 'safety first' tactics were not without their critics.

The returning Newcastle party must have had mixed feelings as they touched down on Tyneside with their 1–1 draw in the bag. Sporting were, after all, the team that had beaten Manchester United 5–0 in 1964, but equally they had lost 2–1 at home to Cardiff City the following year and the Magpies had come so close to emulating that Welsh victory. Amid the confusion it was clear that nothing could be taken for granted.

SECOND ROUND, SECOND LEG

20 November 1968

Newcastle United 1 **Sporting Lisbon 0**

Robson 9

(Newcastle won 2–1 on aggregate)

Newcastle: McFaul, Craig, Clark, Gibb, Burton, Moncur, Scott, Robson, Davies, Elliott, Dyson.

Subs: Bennett, Winstanley, Clarke.

Sporting: Damas, Celestino, Conceiçáo, Goncalves, Armando, Marinho, Pedras, Chico, Lourenco, Carlos, Ernesto.

Subs: Carvalho, Morais, Sitoe.

Attendance: 53,747

Referee: Gerhard Schulenburg (West Germany)

On Monday, 18 November Newcastle supporters awoke to sensational news…Sporting Lisbon's coach Fernando Caiado had resigned. Following on from the draw with Newcastle in the José Alvalade Lisbon had played three League matches and failed to win any of them. A draw with Porto (1–1) was not deemed a disaster, but when it was followed by scoreless draws with Benfica and Belenenses the Sporting management were openly critical of Caiado. The feisty little coach, who had once played with Benfica and the national squad, did not tolerate such criticism, and, despite a key European tie being only 72 hours away, he promptly walked out.

The Sporting coach Caiado.

Thus, although Sporting were able to bring greater experience to the St James' Park fixture they were finding themselves hard-pressed on the domestic front, arguably on the verge of panic, and they ultimately finished a lowly, by their standards, fifth in the Portuguese League. Their general manager was in no doubt that Caiado's actions had been a major blow, and said 'We know the mountainous task we face. The events of the last 24 hours have left their marks.'

The key problem for Sporting, regardless of who was at the helm, was a lack of goals. They actually mustered only 35 in the entire season. Joao Lourenco, the 26-year-old star who had been strangely subdued against Newcastle in Portugal, bagged almost half of them with 15 strikes, and Morais, normally so prolific, had only one League goal to his name by the time of the visit to Tyneside, and even his last-minute goal in the first leg could not mask the disappointment of an injury-ravaged season. Imagine the impact on Tyneside, therefore, when it was

St James' Park main stand.

announced by Sporting Libson's general manager that Morais was not fit enough to start at St James' Park.

Hours before the game it was confirmed that the Morais story was not just a sneaky Continental bluff, it was true and he was not playing. Instead he was on the bench, and given that he had played for Portugal in their wonderful 1966 World Cup team this was a further fillip to the United defence. Indeed, Morais had partnered Eusebio in the fabulous and famous 5–3 win for Portugal over North Korea in one of the World Cup's most celebrated games.

United were also boosted by having won a testing League fixture just four days before this tie. Up against stylish League champions Manchester City, United had risen to the occasion and achieved an impressive 1–0 win. Among the stars had been Bobby Moncur, whom the *Newcastle Chronicle* was able to exclusively reveal had needed a brandy before the game to set him up after recovering from a bout of food poisoning.

For all he may have been weakened by his illness, Moncur lost none of his legendary sharp wit. He had listened to Sporting's tales of woe with some scepticism. 'Their manager is going around town gloomily saying that they haven't a chance. He wants everyone to think they have given up hope. It's all a load of rubbish,' Moncur warned the local press. 'How can a team have no chance when they are going to start the match level at 1–1 and boast a sackful of internationals?'

Eighteen-year-old Keith Dyson was drafted in for Jackie Sinclair, who had been the subject of a £50,000 bid from Blackpool and appeared to be slipping from favour at St James' Park. United took to the field in unfamiliar all-white (there had been comments and criticism about both Newcastle and Lisbon wearing black shorts during the game in Portugal), as Sporting donned their customary green-and-white hoops and black shorts. Even before the game kicked-off there was a scare for Newcastle when Ollie Burton, United's Welsh centre-half, went over on his ankle in the pre-match warm-up. Feeling sheepish and foolish, he informed captain Moncur of his predicament seconds before the start. He told local journalists after the game 'It was all so embarrassing. I felt the searing pain immediately and told Bobby about it as we lined up, and he said just to keep going. I could feel it every time I put my foot down hard.'

Hard but fair play was going to be the order of the evening. The German referee, Gerhard Schulenburg, in the run-up to the tie had made it clear that he would be calling the two captains together before the match with a view to impressing upon them his views on the spirit in which he expected the game to be played. 'Football is a man's game,' he told the press on the eve of the game, 'and I have no objections to it being hard as long as it is also fair. I won't stand for any nonsense and players will have one warning only from me. I've experience of both English and Portuguese football and I know what to expect.'

Perhaps it is over-exaggerating the impact of the managerial change at Sporting, but the massed ranks of the United support seemed to 'sense blood', and by 4.00pm there were queues of expectant fans outside the ground. Amazingly, by the time the match kicked-off at 7.30pm the club had taken record receipts for a home fixture and over 53,000 were packed in under the floodlights. Pity the poor visitors, though, who had left a sunny Lisbon and now found themselves under a grim north-east sky.

Provided Newcastle could avoid conceding a goal at home to Sporting Lisbon, their place in the third round of the Fairs Cup was assured. Their task was as simple and stark as that. And when within the opening 10 minutes, after bouts of intense United pressure, Bryan Robson scored one of the all-time great Newcastle goals, victory looked a distinct possibility.

The goal has entered Tyneside folklore and deservedly so. Robson had been playing table tennis in his spare time and this was reckoned to have

Tommy Gibb.

sharpened his reflexes to such an extent that only Jimmy Greaves appeared sharper around goal. When Tommy Gibb sent a ninth-minute free-kick into the Lisbon penalty area (following a crude foul on young Dyson), it was met by Wyn Davies. The flying Welshman was as good with his head as many players are with their feet and his perfectly cushioned nod allowed Robson to volley home. Given that Robson was a couple of feet off the ground when he lashed the volley goalwards, it is little surprise that the goal enthralled the Geordie crowd.

Indeed, the Magpies had come close to scoring several times before the Robson goal. In the first minute Wyn Davies had tested Damas in the Sporting goal, and then twice in quick succession Jim Scott's trickery enabled him to find space to rifle in powerful drives. When Robson broke the deadlock he scored for the first time in six matches, but even so it was his 14th strike of what proved to be a productive season.

Newcastle might have expected Lisbon to respond vigorously, especially as they needed to score in order to stay in the tie. But the cautious coaching that Caiado had instilled was not easy to shake off and the interim coach, 31-year-old Mario Lino (a one-time full-back with Sporting and Portugal), simply hadn't had enough time to put his own stamp on the side. Thus, although Sporting enjoyed plenty of possession they were more adept at playing square passes than using the probing attacking style needed to penetrate the well-drilled Newcastle defence.

The problem for Sporting Lisbon was that their gameplan had been based on preventing Newcastle scoring on Tyneside and nicking a goal themselves. Their general manager Abraham Sorin had noted after the game in Lisbon that 'We have not thrown in the towel by any means. Actually we are very hopeful. If our defensive systems work well Newcastle United will never score – or will only get one. So much depends on our attack'. Unfortunately for the Portuguese, as noted earlier, this was not the season for Sporting Lisbon to be relying on attacking prowess.

As the game wore on it became increasingly clear that Sporting were toothless in attack. Indeed, in the second half Wyn Davies saw a headed effort mysteriously chalked off when a goal would have killed the tie outright. When Lourenco hobbled off there was more than one journalist who thought that Lisbon's hopes departed the field with him. As it was, the striker who really counted on the night was little Bryan Robson.

In later years Robson modestly credited the goal not to his own prowess but to the confusion that the boisterous Wyn Davies caused in the opposition's defence: 'There was nothing magical about what we did as a team. It was all pretty simple stuff. Not many European sides had faced a player like big Wyn, who really would mix it with his opposite numbers. Joe Harvey was quite clear that we should launch crosses into the box for Wyn and my role was quite simply to scavenge on the bits and pieces he knocked down.'

Lisbon Heroes

JOAO PEDRO MORAIS

Born: Cascais, 6 March 1935.

Career as a player: Sporting Lisbon (1955–69).

Joao Pedro Morais.

The 1963–64 European Cup-Winners' Cup was won by Sporting in a replayed Final, and it was Joao Pedro Morais who scored the only goal of that replay. That he scored it directly from a corner gives some measure of the talents he possessed. He joined Sporting in 1955 and stayed until 1969.

Joao won 10 international caps for Portugal, the first was gained against Scotland on 18 June 1966 at Hampden Park. Portugal won 1–0 that day and both Jim Scott and Jackie Sinclair were playing for Scotland (Sinclair making what would be his only Scotland outing). By a strange twist of fate all three would come together again in the Fairs Cup two years later. Morais won his final cap a year afterwards, so his international career was both brief and intense.

At the 1966 World Cup Finals he was an influential part of the Portuguese squad that finished third. He played in their opening game (a 3–0 win over Hungary at Old Trafford) and in the 3–1 win against Brazil at Goodison, and at the same venue was in the team that won the incredible match against North Korea 5–3, but he missed out on the semi-final against England at Wembley.

HILÁRIO DA CONCEIÇÁO

Born: Mozambique, 19 March 1939.

Career as a player: Sporting Lisbon (1958–73).

Career after football: Ferroviario, Matchedje (coaching 1988–91), youth coach at Sporting (1997–2005).

Like Eusebio, the great Portugal football star of the 1960s, Hilário came from the African nation of Mozambique. A left-sided defender, he won three titles and three national Cups with Sporting but sadly missed out on the European Cup-Winners' Cup triumph when he was sidelined with a broken leg sustained against Vitória Setúbal.

Hilário played in well over 600 games for Sporting and he won 39 caps, the last of which came in the European Championship group of 1971 that Portugal contested with Scotland and Belgium. He was a key part of the 1966 World Cup squad and he played in every game in that tournament.

A coach in Mozambique in the late 1980s, he twice steered clubs to the national Cup. But his heart always lay with the club that had given him his big break, and in 2008 he was the recipient of a presentation when Sporting honoured his 50th anniversary of joining the club. The club chose the occasion of a Sporting versus Barcelona Champions League match to honour one of their favourite sons.

Hilário returned to Britain several times in his career, and a European Cup-Winners' Cup tie against Glasgow Rangers placed him into one of Europe's most bizarre games. Beaten 3–2 in Glasgow, the second leg ended up 4–3 to Sporting. This should have signalled a victory on away goals for Rangers, but the referee did not realise this was the case and ordered a penalty shoot-out! Sporting won the shoot-out and this sparked scenes of great celebration, until 20 minutes later the bad news that Rangers had actually won on away goals was broken to Conceiçáo and his teammates!

VÍTOR DAMAS

Born: Lisbon, 8 October 1947.

Career as a player: Sporting Lisbon (1962–76), Racing Santander (1976–81), Vitoria Guimaraes (1981–83), Sporting Lisbon (1984–89).

Career after football: Coach at Sporting (1989–2003).

Vítor Damas.

One of the finest Portuguese goalkeepers of all time, Vítor was renowned for his wonderful reflexes. He won 29 caps in total as well as two League titles and three Portuguese Cups. No Sporting player has made more appearances for the club than the rather grandly named Vítor Manuel Afonso Damas de Oliveira.

Vítor turned out against England at Wembley in December 1969 and was described in the match programme thus: 'Spectacular, stylish, occasionally over-confident'. He made classic progress through the ranks at Sporting, won 10 Portugal Youth caps and turned out against England Under-23s before taking his place in the full squad aged 22 against Mexico. Both at domestic level and in the international side he had to oust the vastly experienced Carvalho from the number-one jersey.

Damas was with Sporting for 14 years before he moved to Spain with Racing Santander. The longevity of his career was put down to his excellent training methods and he was able to play two matches in the 1986 World Cup finals in Mexico when standing in for an injured teammate.

Vítor was only 55 when he died of cancer in 2003.

Second Round Results in Full

Aberdeen *v.* Real Zaragoza	2–1	0–3	2–4
AIK (Stockholm) *v.* Hannover 96	4–2	2–5	6–7
Aris (Salonika) *v.* Újpest Dozsa	1–2	1–9	2–11
Chelsea *v.* DWS (Amsterdam)	0–0	0–0	0–0 x aet

FC Hansa Rostock *v.* AC Fiorentina	3–2	1–2	4–4*
Göztepe *v.* FC Arges (Pitesti)	3–0	2–3	5–3
Hamburger SV *v.* Slavia Prague	4–1	1–3	5–4
Hibernian *v.* 1.FC Lokomotive Leipzig	3–1	1–0	4–1
Juventus *v.* Eintracht Frankfurt	0–0	0–1	0–1 aet
KSV Waregem *v.* Legia Warsaw	1–0	0–2	1–2
Leeds United *v.* SSC Napoli	2–0	0–2	2–2 x aet
OFK Belgrade *v.* Bologna	1–0	1–1	2–1
Panathinaikos *v.* Athletic Bilbao	0–0	0–1	0–1
Rangers *v.* Dundalk	6–1	3–0	9–1
Sporting CP (Lisbon) *v.* **Newcastle United**	1–1	0–1	1–2
Vitória Setúbal *v.* Olympique Lyonnais	5–0	2–1	7–1

x Leeds United and DWS (Amsterdam) progressed on a coin toss.

* Indicates a win on the away goals rule.

A Three-Horse Race

Traditionally three clubs fight out the Portuguese title, and in 1969 Sporting were just behind Benfica in terms of success. From the start of the Portuguese League in 1934 through to 1969, the top four clubs in Portugal were as follows:

	P	W	D	L	F	A	Pts
Benfica	798	558	127	113	2437	969	1243
Sporting	798	535	130	133	2370	951	1200
Porto	798	484	129	185	2047	1070	1097
Belenenses	798	418	150	230	1820	1089	986

Real Zaragoza

Spanish Thriller on New Year's Day

THIRD ROUND, FIRST LEG

1 January 1969

Real Zaragoza 3 **Newcastle United 2**

Santos 4, Bustillo 14, Planas II 57 *Robson 7, Davies 32*

Newcastle: McFaul, Craig, Clark, Gibb, Burton, Moncur, Dyson, Robson, Davies, Scott, Foggon.

Subs: Clarke, McNamee, Sinclair.

Real Zaragoza: Nieves, Borras, Irusquieta, Planas II, Santamaria, Santos, Moya, Gonzales, Bustillo, Marcelino, Martin.

Subs: Violeta, Planas I, Diaz.

Attendance: 22,000

Referee: A. Ott (West Germany)

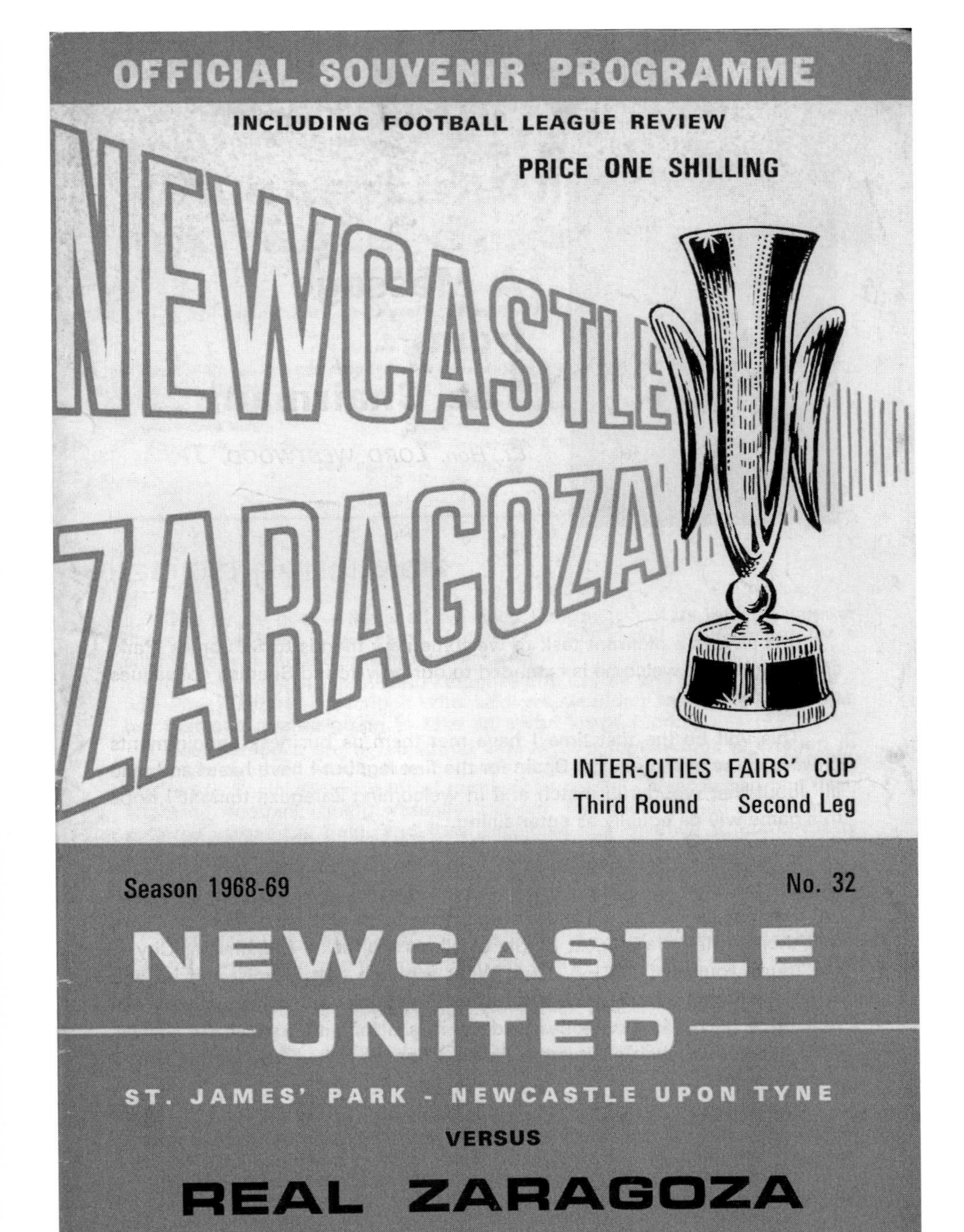
OFFICIAL SOUVENIR PROGRAMME
INCLUDING FOOTBALL LEAGUE REVIEW
PRICE ONE SHILLING
NEWCASTLE
ZARAGOZA
INTER-CITIES FAIRS' CUP
Third Round Second Leg
Season 1968-69
No. 32
NEWCASTLE UNITED
ST. JAMES' PARK - NEWCASTLE UPON TYNE
VERSUS
REAL ZARAGOZA
Wednesday, 15th January, 1969
Kick-off 7-30 p.m.

So here was another test against former European winners and another Iberian test at that. This time Spanish club Real Zaragoza lay in store and they could point to having won the trophy as recently as 1964; what is more they had contested the 1966 Final too. Curiously, both of their Finals had been all-Spanish affairs: victory in 1964 had come against Valencia in Barcelona (a single-game Final) and then they experienced the other side of the coin with defeat over two legs against Barcelona in 1966.

Real Zaragoza also had considerable experience of British football. They had earned a reputation as 'the Hammer of the Scots' and had enjoyed contests with English sides too; putting both Everton and Leeds United to the sword in previous years. Their qualities were admired by audiences across Europe and they had a reputation for playing precision football. Yet for all that class Zaragoza had only won on away goals in the first round against little-known Bulgarian opponents FC Trakia of Plovdiv.

In round two Zaragoza had made a trip to the north-east; albeit the north-east of Scotland. Pitched up against Aberdeen they performed well, losing narrowly at Pittodrie Stadium when a late headed goal by Jose Antonio Tejedor gave them hope for the return in Spain. Tejedor was on target again in the second leg at the famous Romareda Stadium, but it was two members of the Zaragoza *'los Magnificos'* – a particularly talented forward line – in Marcelino Martinez and Juan Manuel Villa who did the real damage. The 3–0 Zaragoza win saw off yet another British challenge and an inexperienced Aberdeen team with ease.

The Zaragoza side that edged out Aberdeen consisted of: Nieves, Rico, Rija, Violeta, Gonzales, Borras, Tejedor, Santos, Marcelino, Villa and Lapetra. By the time the men from Spain were due to face Newcastle there were significant alterations from that side, with no fewer than eight changes made to the XI that had dumped Aberdeen. Interestingly, the Spaniards had been forced to substitute both full-backs, and so Bustillo and Planas II were introduced. But change was probably necessary for Zaragoza as they were not having a good season and languished in the lower half of the Spanish League.

REAL PROGRESS

Round	Opponents	Res.	Scorers
1 A	Trakia Plovdiv (Bulgaria)	L 1–3	Tejedor
1 H	Trakia Plovdiv	W 2–0	Bustillo (2)
2 A	Aberdeen (Scotland)	L 1–2	Tejedor
2 H	Aberdeen	W 3–0	Marcelino, Tejedor, Villa

Quite bluntly Zaragoza were struggling near the foot of La Liga. From the first six games of the season they gathered only four points and Barcelona had lashed in four goals against them. Meanwhile, United's preparations had perhaps benefited with away fixtures to Queens Park Rangers and Leeds United in the run-up to this tie. The match in the capital was against the League's strugglers, and the West London club ended the season rooted to the foot of the table. Nevertheless, they gave United a testing time in the capital and a 1–1 draw resulted. A few days later, on Boxing Day, Newcastle travelled to Leeds to face Don Revie's excellent team. In front of a crowd of 44,995 Newcastle found themselves under the cosh for long periods and perhaps facing the kind of sustained pressure they could expect in Zaragoza. A 2–1 defeat had been no disgrace.

Bizarrely, the Inter-Cities tie was scheduled to take place on New Year's Day. Thus the United players brought in their quietest ever New Year before trotting out at the La Romareda Stadium, traditionally one of the more noisy and hostile of Spanish venues. La Romareda had been opened in September 1957 with a match against Osasuna, and it was very much a traditional Continental ground. So much so that even by 1969 only the main stand had a roof. Set in an open square on a main artery into the city, it was a stark, concreted stadium, known to be ferociously hot in the summer and icy cold in the winter. For the United match there were 22,000 fans present on a freezing day; arguably more akin to a Tyneside winter than the typical image of the Iberian peninsular.

Ollie Burton.

The Spaniards were vastly experienced at this level and showed their class by going ahead in only the fourth minute. Following a corner-kick Iam McFaul managed to beat out a Bustillo header, but he had no answer as experienced left-half Santos drove in the rebound from around the 15-yard mark. It was imperative that United hit back and calmed the excitable Portuguese crowd. Amazingly, they did so within three minutes. Tommy Gibb was the architect, ending a four-man move by 'worming' his way along the byline before cutting the ball back expertly for the ever-alert Robson to despatch the ball into the Zaragoza net.

The football at this stage of the game was exhilarating, and before quarter of an hour had elapsed Bustillo restored Zaragoza's lead. Alan Foggon was penalised for a rash tackle on the tricky right-winger Francisco Moya, and when Borras flighted over a tantalising free-kick it was the irrepressible Bustillo who headed home from five yards. Soon afterwards another free-kick brought United level. Gibb floated a cross over and the robust Wyn Davies climbed highest to head home.

Few had predicted four goals in the opening half and it was clear that the away goals would serve United well, but they were behind again in the

Wyn Davies.

57th minute when Planas II glanced home a stunning goal following wonderful work by the talented winger Armando Martin, who had 'skinned' two defenders in the build-up.

Planas' goal was the end of the scoring and United knew that while they would face an uphill struggle back on Tyneside they had laid the foundations to progress yet further. They had made good use of the generously proportioned pitch in Zaragoza (it measured 118 x 74 yards) and quelled the threat of Marcelino in particular – the man who had sunk Hearts, Dundee and Aberdeen.

THIRD ROUND, SECOND LEG

15 January 1969

Newcastle United 2 — **Real Zaragoza 1**

Robson 3, Gibb 28 — *Martin 42*

(Newcastle won on away goals ruling)

Newcastle: McFaul, Craig, Clark, Gibb, Burton, Moncur, Scott, Robson, Davies, Dyson, Foggon.

Subs: Guthrie, McNamee, Clarke.

Real Zaragoza: Nieves, Rico, Irusquieta, Gonzales, Santamaria, Borras, Martin, Violeta, Bustillo, Santos, Fontenia.

Subs: Alarcia, Tejedor.

Attendance: 56,055

Referee: M. Barde (France)

ZARAGOZA AGAINST BRITISH OPPOSITION

Season	Comp.	Opponents	H	A	Decider
1962–63	FC	Glentoran	6–0	2–0	
1964–65	CWC	Dundee	2–1	2–2	
		Cardiff City	2–2	1–0	
		West Ham Utd	1–1	1–2	
1965–66	FC	Hearts	2–2	3–3	1–0
		Dunfermline	4–2	0–1	
		Leeds Utd	1–0	1–2	1–3
1966–67	CWC	Everton	2–0	0–1	
		Rangers	2–0	0–2	**
1968–69	FC	Aberdeen	3–0	1–2	

** – *lost on toss of a coin*

When Zaragoza were drawn against Newcastle it was the 11th time they had faced British opposition. In their 10 previous clashes they had progressed seven times and been knocked out on three occasions.

Zaragoza's first British challenge surfaced in the Fairs Cup in 1962 when they were drawn against Northern Ireland's Glentoran, but a comfortable 8–0 aggregate win heralded the safe passage of the Spaniards. But it was in 1964–65 that they first really grabbed the attention of the footballing public on these shores. In that year's Cup-Winners' Cup they completed their British odyssey by playing the proverbial trio of Scotsmen, Welshmen and Englishmen. First up for Zaragoza were Scotland's Dundee, and after a 2–2 draw on Tayside the Spanish side won 2–1 at home. That result carried them through to a clash with Cardiff City, and after winning 1–0 at Ninian Park the job was completed with a

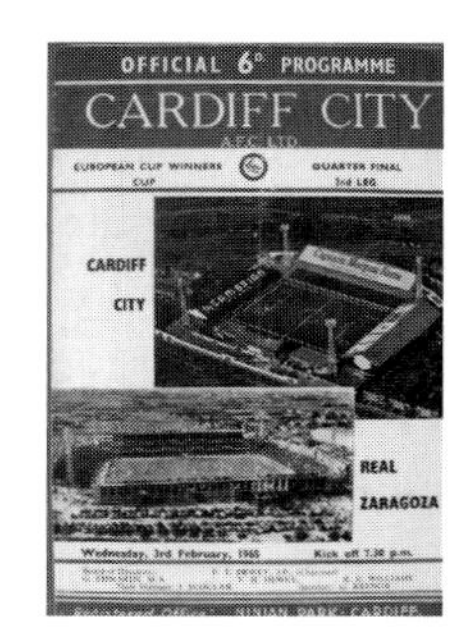

compelling 2–2 draw in Spain. Finally, the men from Zaragoza came unstuck when they met West Ham United. Beaten 2–1 in London's East End they could not reverse the tie at home and a 1–1 draw took the Londoners through and, indeed, on their way to the trophy.

There was no respite for Zaragoza in the following season. That time the Inter-Cities Fairs Cup was the competition in question and their British adventure again brought three clashes on these shores. It all began in the capital of Scotland against Heart of Midlothian. A sumptuous fare was served up by both sides in a remarkable 3–3 draw, and when the sides tied 2–2 in Spain the match required a replay (the game was played before away goals counted double), and in the re-match Zaragoza clinched a 1–0 victory.

Barely had the Spanish team touched base again before they were sent back to Scotland to face Dunfermline Athletic. Beaten 1–0 in Fife, it took an impressive 4–2 home win to reverse the tie. That was at the quarter-final stage, and in the semis Leeds United barred Zaragoza's passage. At home Zaragoza won 1–0 but they were beaten 2–1 in Yorkshire and so again a third match was required. This time the result was more emphatic and Leeds advanced courtesy of a 3–1 triumph.

That surely ought to have been the end of Zaragoza's contact with the British Isles...but no! In the 1966–67 Cup-Winners' Cup they pulled Everton out of the hat and advanced courtesy of a 2–0 home win following a 1–0 away defeat. It was Rangers who halted their progress in that year's competition. Both sides won their home matches 2–0 but rather than decide things by a third match it was decreed that the toss of a coin would suffice and Rangers won through.

TOP OF THE CHARTS

Ob-la-Di Ob-La-Da
Marmalade
Lily the Pink
Scaffold
Build Me Up Buttercup
The Foundations
Albatross
Fleetwood Mac
I'm The Urban Spaceman
Bonzo Dog Doo-Dah Band
Sabre Dance
Love Sculpture
Ain't Got No
Nina Simone
1-2-3 O'Leary
Des O'Connor
Son of A Preacher Man
Dusty Springfield
Something's Happening
Herman's Hermits

Unbeaten at home in that long, proud run, Zaragoza would be a stiff challenge and so it proved.

The task facing Joe Harvey's men was quite simple. Above every clarion call for a performance, for focus and for drive, they quite simply required a goal to progress. Wonderfully, and ecstatically, United grabbed just what they needed in only the third minute of the game.

When the goal arrived it came from a reliable source. Ollie Burton sent Bryan Robson off on one of his trademark runs, and when the tricky little forward had tied the opposition in knots he unleashed a wonderful 30-yard drive that simply ripped beyond Nieves and into the roof of the Zaragoza net. It was the third time in the competition that Robson had netted in the opening 10 minutes of a tie.

Zaragoza's goalkeeper Nieves was a key figure as the night wore on. He was badly at fault as United went 2–0 up, poorly punching a Robson corner and finding himself hopelessly marooned as Tommy Gibb sent a gentle header into the unguarded net. His nightmare ended just 60 seconds later when he was injured in a clash with Alan Foggon and stretchered off to be replaced by Alarcia. Rarely have the gods of good fortune shone so brightly on one team as they did at this point on Newcastle.

A 2–0 half-time lead would have been ideal for Newcastle, but it was not to be. In a sweet flowing move Irusquieta crossed and Santos and Martin combined before right-winger Martin swept the ball home. United were up against it and the sense of dread deepened when David Craig was injured and had to be replaced by Ron Guthrie. Then, in a bizarre twist, Guthrie himself was injured and replaced by John McNamee. When Keith Dyson was also injured Newcastle had exhausted their options from the bench and the instruction went out to Dyson that he would have to soldier on.

The second half was a nerve-jangling affair, and while United had chances to extend their lead they also lived dangerously on a few occasions. However, the final whistle came with United still 2–1 to the good, and a 4–4 aggregate score was good enough to see United progress on the new away goals ruling.

'The fates' had perhaps been on Newcastle's side. Real were undoubtedly significantly hampered by not having Marcelino to call upon. Ordinarily Bustillo would have been an adequate replacement, but his season was compromised by the fact that after he had achieved a dream move to Barcelona, and he had then been loaned back to Zaragoza in order to complete his National Service. The Spaniards were also rattled by Newcastle's physical approach to the game, and their delay in appearing for the second half was apparently due to a fierce tactical row in the away dressing

Tommy Gibb.

room. Having said that, Zaragoza knew how to 'put themselves about' and skipper Santos and Borras were both booked in the tense second half.

The 1968–69 season was actually a good one in which to draw the Spanish Cup experts. The final League table from that campaign shows clearly that Zaragoza were a spent force by 1969. Only a slender single-point margin saved them from the drop, which was a considerable turn around in fortunes for a side used to a top-six finish. In the 1970–71 season Zaragoza finally hit rock bottom and they were relegated, having finished at the foot of La Liga with only three wins all season.

La Liga 1968–69 final table

P	Club	Pld	W	D	L	GF	GA	Pts
1	Real Madrid	30	18	11	1	46	21	**47**
2	UD Las Palmas	30	15	8	7	45	34	**38**
3	Barcelona	30	13	10	7	40	18	**36**
4	CD Sabadell	30	10	12	18	33	34	**32**
5	Valencia	30	10	11	9	36	39	**31**
6	Atlético Madrid	30	10	10	10	40	37	**30**
7	Real Sociedad	30	10	9	11	36	33	**29**
8	Granada	30	11	7	12	26	38	**29**
9	Elche F	30	7	15	8	25	23	**29**
10	Deportivo de La Coruña	30	11	6	13	39	44	**28**
11	Atlético Bilbao	30	10	8	12	42	46	**28**
12	Pontevedra	30	7	13	10	20	23	**27**
13	**Zaragoza**	**30**	**8**	**10**	**12**	**36**	**36**	**26**
14	Málaga	30	9	7	14	37	42	**25**
15	RCD Español	30	8	8	14	29	36	**24**
16	Córdoba	30	5	11	14	31	57	**21**

Zaragoza Heroes

MIGUEL ÁNGEL BUSTILLO LAFOZ

Born: Zaragoza, 9 September 1946.

Career as a player: Real Zaragoza (1967–69), Barcelona (1969–72), Malaga (1972–77).

Miguel Ángel Bustillo Lafoz.

Signed from Third Division Spanish football in 1967, Miguel Ángel Bustillo Lafoz enjoyed a remarkable season in 1968–69. He was transferred to Barcelona in the summer of 1968 with Real Zaragoza receiving £50,000 plus two players. But within weeks Barcelona sent Bustillo out on loan – remarkably to Zaragoza – perhaps motivated by the player's requirement to serve his National Service near Zaragoza. It was well known at the time of his move that the Zaragoza president Alfonso Usar was resigned to selling him, and in getting both Oliveras and Borras in the same deal he did his club proud.

Bustillo played only 60 games for Zaragoza but in grabbing 28 goals he won the fans' adulation. Surprisingly he only won five caps for Spain, which considering his technique and strength was a real surprise.

ELEUTERIO SANTOS BRITO

Born: Tenerife, 9 November 1940.

Career as a player: Tenerife (1960–63), Real Zaragoza (1963–71), C.D. Tudelano (1972).

Eleuterio Santos Brito.

It seems remarkable that Santos won just a single international cap (in Malmö against Sweden in 1968). When he joined Zaragoza in March 1963 it cost a whopping 1,675,000 pesetas to take him to the mainland. Tall, dark-haired and extremely direct, he seemed to be the epitome of the new athletic footballer breaking through.

Santos made his debut with CD Tenerife in the 1959–60 season and quickly caught the eye of bigger clubs. His transfer to Zaragoza was a key part of establishing the 'Magnificent Five' forward line, and he rewarded his new club with a steady stream of goals. The statistics are impressive. In both 1964 and 1966 he helped Zaragoza win the Spanish Cup and he was an extremely popular player with supporters. He scored 56 La Liga goals in 183 starts, in Europe he scored 12 goals in 38 matches and in all he scored 98 times for Zaragoza from 284 outings.

He left Zaragoza when he was 31 and supporters were stunned when he died in January 2008 aged just 67 back in his beloved Tenerife.

MARCELINO MARTINEZ CAO

Born: La Coruña, 29 April 1940.

Career as a player: Racing de Ferrol (1957), Real Zaragoza (1958–69).

When Spain won the 1964 European Championship Final against Russia it was Marcelino who scored the winning goal with a header that

Marcelino Martinez Cao.

entered Spanish footballing folklore. Something of a nightmare for British and in particular Scottish defences, he had scored the winner against Hearts in the dramatic 1965–66 Fairs Cup match and then in the next round netted against Dunfermline. A couple of years later he was on target against Aberdeen as Zaragoza advanced to the Newcastle tie. He had been the cutting edge of the Real forward line that was known as 'The Magnificent Five' – Carnario, Santos, Marcelino, Villa and Lapetra.

Marcelino joined Real when he was only 19 and scored 71 League goals in 226 outings and 117 goals in all Zaragoza matches. He was capped 14 times by Spain and scored four goals (two of them against the Republic of Ireland). As clever and innovative off the field as he was effective on it, among his off-field successes were a fleet of fishing boats and clever financial investments. He needed that business acumen because he was lost to the game through injury from the age of 29, and his early retirement played a huge part in Zaragoza's later problems.

Forty-four years on from his winning goal against Russia he was in huge demand for interviews as Spain contested (and won) the European Championship in Switzerland/Austria. A goal by Fernando Torres saw the mantle of last Spaniard to score the winning goal in a major tournament finally shifted elsewhere!

Third Round Results in Full

Athletic Bilbao *v.* Eintracht Frankfurt	1–0	1–1	2–1
DWS (Amsterdam) *v.* Rangers	0–2	1–2	1–4
Hamburger SV *v.* Hibernian	1–0	1–2	2–2*
Leeds United *v.* Hannover 96	5–1	2–1	7–2
Legia Warsaw *v.* Újpest Dozsa	0–1	2–2	2–3
OFK Belgrade *v.* Göztepe	3–1	0–2	3–3*
Real Zaragoza *v.* **Newcastle United**	3–2	1–2	4–4*
Vitória FC (Setúbal) *v.* AC Fiorentina	3–0	1–2	4–2

* Newcastle United, Hamburger SV and Göztepe all won on away goals.

Vitória Setúbal

A Sense of Déjà vu!

QUARTER-FINAL, FIRST LEG

12 March 1969

Newcastle United 5 **Vitória Setúbal 1**

Foggon 23, Robson 36, 75, Davies 60, Gibb 89 *Jose Maria 84*

Newcastle: McFaul, Craggs, Clark, Gibb, Burton, Moncur, Robson, Horsfield, Davies, Scott, Foggon.

Subs: Sinclair, McNamee, Clarke.

Setúbal: Vital, Herculano, Caricco, Wagner, Cardoso, Alfredo, Batista, Jose Maria, Figueiredo, Arcanjo, Joao.

Subs: Petita, Tomé.

Attendance: 57,662

Referee: Mr Curt Liedberg (Sweden)

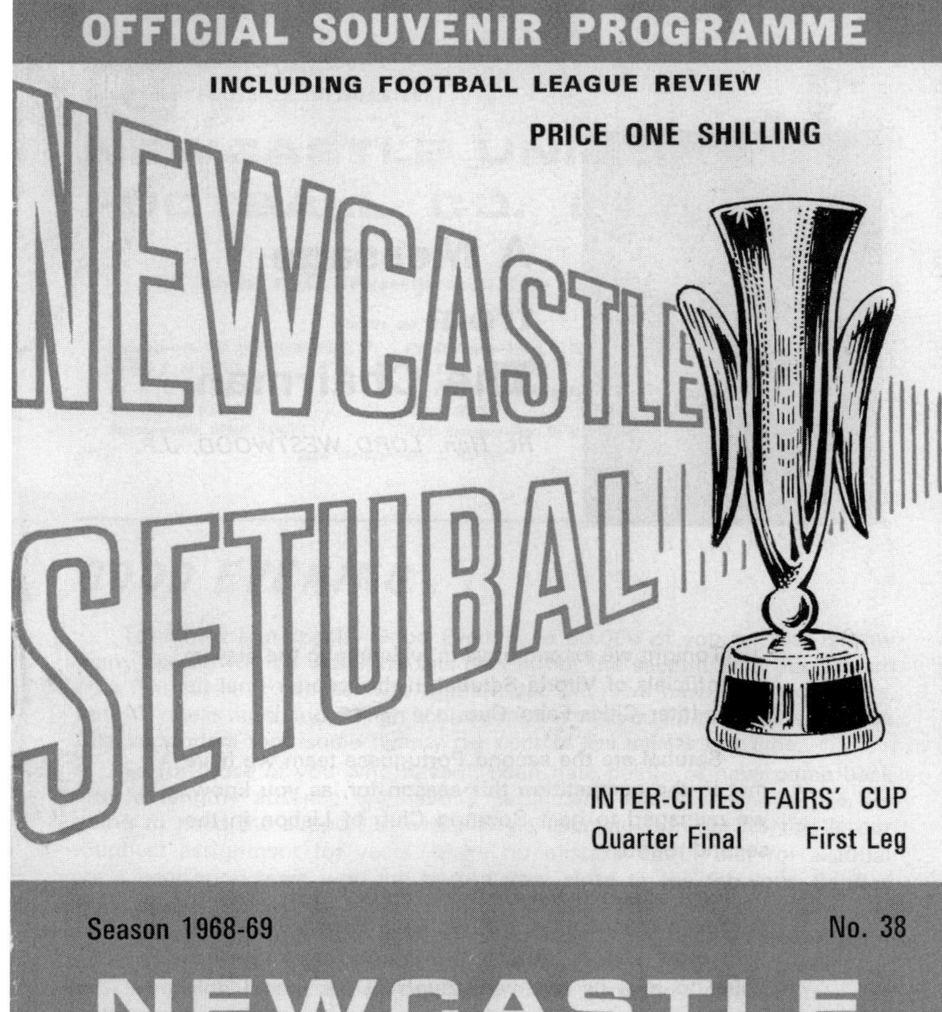
OFFICIAL SOUVENIR PROGRAMME
INCLUDING FOOTBALL LEAGUE REVIEW
PRICE ONE SHILLING
NEWCASTLE
SETUBAL
INTER-CITIES FAIRS' CUP
Quarter Final First Leg
Season 1968-69
No. 38
NEWCASTLE
UNITED
ST. JAMES' PARK - NEWCASTLE UPON TYNE
VERSUS
VITORIA SETUBAL
Wednesday, 12th March, 1969
Kick-off 7-30 p.m.

Newcastle's Iberian adventure was set to continue in the quarter-finals. This time Portuguese side Vitória Setúbal lay in wait. It promised to be a tough test for United as Setúbal had won their national Cup twice in the previous three years (1965 and 1967) and even had a limited European history. But it was their performances in the 1968–69 Fairs Cup campaign that had made others sit up and take notice.

To reach Tyneside Setúbal had beaten Linfield, Lyon and Fiorentina. Neither the Irish nor the French side had been expected to halt Vitória (Lyon were a pale shadow of the force they are now) and so it had proved. Against the Belfast-based Linfield the quicksilver forwards of Setúbal had scored three times both at home and away. In Portugal goals by Tomé, Figueiredo and Caricco had all but killed the tie, and in Northern Ireland Setúbal scored three times in the first half through Figueiredo (again), Batista and Arcanjo to ease through. Lyon never rose to the challenge, but Fiorentina had been expected to bar Setúbal's progress, and the crushing victory over the Italian giants set down a real marker. Drawn at home for the third successive tie, Setúbal won a thrilling game 3–0 which meant that a 2–1 reversal in Italy did little damage.

The Vitória Setúbal side that faced Newcastle at St James' Park.

For all that recent strength, Setúbal were by no means one of Portugal's biggest clubs. They lagged some way behind the likes of Benfica, Porto and Sporting Lisbon, and since their foundation in 1910 they had enjoyed something of a chequered history. Based in a small town just south of Lisbon, they had a population of only 60,000 to call upon, and therefore playing to crowds of less than 10,000 was the norm. Managed by Fernando Vaz, who had managed Portugal for a few games as well as the national army side, Setúbal had been relegated twice in recent history but each time Vaz had led them back to the top flight.

As well as the Cup triumphs of 1965 and 1967 he had also taken Setúbal to the 1966 and 1968 Cup Finals, and thus their reputation was made as doughty cup campaigners. But they played an expansive game in a hot region of the country, and their stadium reflected their background – a typical European-style open bowl where fans were more used to basking in the sunshine than shivering in wind and rain.

It was perhaps fortunate, therefore, that it snowed when Setúbal arrived in Newcastle. It has been said that the Setúbal players were so shocked and delighted by the blanket of white that they asked press photographers to step outside the hotel with them and take their pictures in the snow. It was still snowing when the game kicked-off and this clearly unsettled an otherwise competent Portuguese side. Unprepared for such weather, they did not even have the luxury of donning gloves; although Jacinto Joao improvised cleverly by wearing a pair of socks on his hands.

The big loss for Setúbal was Conceiçáo; the club captain's steady and dependable presence was significant, but his dismissal in the previous round against Fiorentina meant he had to sit out the first-leg. Newcastle too were forced to make changes for this game. In came John Craggs at right-back and Arthur Horsfield at inside-right. There was also a slight issue with confidence. Since late January United had played five fixtures and had won only one match, and they had also been bundled out of the FA Cup. Manchester City had beaten Newcastle in the FA Cup, containing United in front of just under 58,000 in the home Cup tie then administering the coup de grace at Maine Road. Clearly, the Inter-Cities Fairs Cup was looking like becoming the club's salvation in an otherwise disappointing season.

February had been disrupted by weather, but at Southampton United had failed to score and then at West Ham United the Magpies had slipped to a 3–1 defeat. The only bright spot had come four days before the Setúbal game when Newcastle beat Burnley 1–0 at St James' Park.

Fortunately, the European tie at St James' Park was another personal triumph for Bryan Robson. His brace of goals and all-out industry was one of the main dynamics in United's showing. After a testing opening, in which Setúbal gradually settled to a dangerous game on the break, Newcastle scored the vital opening goal through young Alan Foggon. The 19-year-old became the youngest-ever Magpie to score in a senior game with his strike, and he would feature later in the competition too.

John Craggs.

Foggon's 23rd-minute headed opener, which came from a cross by young right-back John Craggs, settled any Gallowgate nerves and in the 36th minute Robson scored the first of his two goals. Again Craggs was the provider as the plucky full-back picked himself up after being fouled and swung over an inviting, curving cross. Caricco made a hash of a headed clearance and

Robson rammed home the loose ball. Robson, with his low centre of gravity, was clearly revelling in the inclement conditions. Two-nil up at half-time Newcastle were nevertheless desperate for a third goal to give them some leeway for the return leg in Portugal. But before the second half could begin, the St James' groundstaff had to go round the pitch markings with red dye to make the lines visible against the snow.

The players emerged shivering for the second period with the likes of Wyn Davies and Vitor Batista donning gloves that had been rustled up from somewhere. After 55 minutes a clearly freezing Arcanjo was replaced by Petita. Arcanjo, a devastating speed-master on his day, was simply frozen and completely out of sorts.

In the 59th minute Davies scored when Robson knocked-on a Clark cross that provoked dramatic protests from Setúbal. The Swedish official Curt Liedberg was surrounded by Portuguese defenders and was persuaded to consult his linesman, but neither official had seen any infringement and the goal stood. It was later revealed that such was the manhandling that Liedberg suffered from the Portuguese players the collar of his jacket was ripped. As the *Daily Express* saw things it was a bizarre protest: 'The one uproar of the night followed Newcastle's third goal when centre-forward Davies netted from four yards and the Setúbal players almost carried the Swedish referee Curt Leidberg to a linesman in a vain appeal for offside'.

John Gibson of the *Newcastle Chronicle* was a deal more pointed in his observations: 'Setúbal's footballers, who had created such a friendly atmosphere during their stay on Tyneside, left a bad taste after an explosive incident in the 60th minute last night. Their disgraceful manhandling of Swedish referee Leidberg after Setúbal had claimed Wyn Davies was offside when he scored left me astonished and dismayed. The blond, burly Leidberg was set upon by five Setúbal defenders and carried

Bryan 'Pop' Robson.

bodily to the touchline for a consultation with linesman Ewart Fargh that he didn't want. When he tried to object his collar was torn and his neck badly scratched. Several people I spoke to afterwards felt that the referee should have sent off at least two Setúbal players but such a decision would have sparked off a near riot and the match might not have finished.'

There was a frantic finale to the game. With 15 minutes to go Robson scored a fourth when Vital fluffed a Clark free-kick, and that seemed to win the tie outright. Credit was due to Vitória Setúbal, however, for while they must have been praying for the end they mustered a late rally and scored an away goal. Six minutes from time their centre-forward Figueiredo set off on a run that saw him beat three Newcastle defenders before squaring a lovely pass in front of Jose Maria. He in turn drove the ball high into the net, leaving McFaul helpless. It was the best goal of the evening and showed exactly why Setúbal had invested so much time in luring him from Angola.

Setúbal promptly sought a second to try and make a real contest of the second leg. They introduced Tomé (a hat-trick hero in the 5–1 thrashing of Lyon earlier in the tournament) for Jacinto Joao and Newcastle countered by bringing on Sinclair for Horsfield. At last there was some fire in the Portuguese play and for a few brief minutes Newcastle were put firmly on the back foot. But as Setúbal pushed for that second goal they were naïvely exposing their defence, and Tommy Gibb's final-minute counter killed the tie stone dead. A half clearance in the Setúbal penalty area fell to Gibb and from around 22 yards the former Partick Thistle man hit a low drive home.

Such was the scale of this win that few could disagree with the summary in *The Times* that stated '...this was a handsome victory and almost certainly books Newcastle a place in the semi-finals'. The Newcastle skipper, Bobby Moncur, told a waiting pressman that 'It will be our own fault if we don't reach the semi-final now but we mustn't be complacent. Setúbal will play good football out there and they aren't a bad side despite this result'.

Fernando Vaz, the Setúbal boss, was realistic in the aftermath, and said 'We will get our revenge in Lisbon, but four goals is asking a lot. When we arrived at St James' Park and saw the pitch we knew we had no chance. And the shocking offside goal of Davies at such a crucial time really did for us. It was actually like a three-hour stint for us, our muscles aren't used the torture of playing in the snow back home.'

QUARTER-FINAL, SECOND LEG

26 March 1969

Vitória Setúbal 3 **Newcastle United 1**

Arcanjo 27, Petita 60, Figueiredo 66 *Davies 40*

(Newcastle won 6–4 on aggregate)

Setúbal: Vital, Conceiçáo, Caricco, Wagner, Cardoso, Alfredo, Batista, Jose Maria, Figueiredo, Arcanjo, Joao.

Subs: Petita, Torres.

Newcastle: McFaul, Craggs, Clark, Gibb, Burton, Moncur, Sinclair, Robson, Davies, Scott, Foggon.

Subs: McNamee, Elliott, Hope.

Attendance: 34,000

Referee: Mr Othmar Huber (Switzerland)

Four days after a gruelling Tyne-Wear derby Newcastle were put through the mill by a very physical Setúbal side. Mind you, the derby game with Sunderland was perhaps the ideal preparation. United scored after 12 minutes against their local rivals through Jackie Sinclair and then dominated the match, looked comfortable and were actually in easy street when Colin Suggett popped up eight minutes from time to equalise. Suddenly it was 'game on' once more and in the final minute Pop Robson banged a shot off the junction of post and crossbar.

TOP OF THE CHARTS

Where Do You Go To My Lovely
Peter Sarstedt

I Heard It Through The Grapevine
Marvin Gaye

The Way It used To Be
Engelbert Humperdink

Surround Yourself With Sorrow
Cilla Black

Gentle on My Mind
Dean Martin

First of May
Bee Gees

Monsieur Dupont
Sandi Shaw

Wichita Lineman
Glen Campbell

I'm Gonna Make You Love Me
Diana Ross and the Supremes and the Temptations

Please Don't Go
Donald Peers

One pleasing aspect of the north-east clash was that everyone came through with a clean bill of health, so not only had United been tested to the full but the same side could be selected for their following game.

The feisty manager of Setúbal, Fernando Vaz, had accused Newcastle of being rough on Tyneside and at times it seemed as though there was an element of revenge on Setúbal's minds as they tore into Newcastle from the off. But with a four-goal advantage it was going to take a fightback of historic proportions to knock United out. But how Setúbal pushed for that dramatic outcome.

Frank Clark.

The only hope for the Portuguese side was to call upon their greater European experience and their near mythical home form. They had first tasted European football in 1962–63 when they played in the Cup-Winners' Cup but lost heavily away to St Etienne. In 1965 they contested the Cup-Winners' Cup again but this time lost to Danish side Aarhus, and one year on they lost in the first round of the Fairs Cup, this time to the mighty Juventus. But 1967 brought them their first Euro victory, albeit against little Fredrikstad before they were crushed by Bayern Munich, conceding six goals in Bavaria.

However, domestically there was no doubt that Setúbal were enjoying something of a golden era. They were regularly supplying a clutch of players to the international side and were contesting one of the tightest ever Portuguese title chases. It was only narrow but costly away defeats to both Benfica and Porto that denied Setúbal the Championship. Just how good Setúbal were can be gauged from the fact that they did not lose a match at home all season and only away defeats at the top clubs meant that they finished in fourth place, four points behind the impressive Benfica side which had contested the previous season's European Cup.

Final Portuguese 1968–69 table:

Club		**P**	**W**	**D**	**L**	**F**	**A**	**Pts**
1	Benfica	26	16	7	3	49	17	39
2	FC Porto	26	15	7	4	39	23	37
3	VSC Guimarães	26	13	10	3	46	17	36
4	**VFC Setúbal**	**26**	**13**	**9**	**4**	**45**	**20**	**35**
5	Sporting Lisbon	26	11	8	7	35	20	30
6	Académica	26	12	6	8	48	32	30
7	GD CUF	26	8	11	7	32	30	27
8	Belenenses	26	8	10	8	31	33	26
9	Varzim SC	26	7	8	11	32	49	22
10	UFCI Tomar	26	7	7	12	27	47	21
11	Leixões SC	26	7	7	12	21	30	21
12	Sporting Braga	26	6	7	13	20	47	19
13	Atlético	26	5	2	19	26	49	12
14	AD Sanjoanense	26	3	3	20	15	52	9

United stayed at the Palácio Hotel in Estoril and were in relaxed mood before the tie. This was despite the fact that the fixture would not be being played in Setúbal, rather it was to be moved to the José Alvalade Stadium in Lisbon. Astonishingly, this meant that in the same competition United would be returning to a stadium where they had contested an earlier round. Setúbal's own ground (the Estádio Do Bonfim) was undergoing reconstruction – despite having been opened as recently as 1962 – and was without floodlighting, so the switch to Lisbon made sense.

For Setúbal's supporters it meant a day out in Lisbon and the game carried something of a carnival atmosphere with neither side being truly at home. It is always worth repeating and emphasising that

Setúbal was home to a population of only around 60,000 people, which makes their loyal support of around 10,000 all the more remarkable.

The Portuguese side welcomed back their right-back Conceiçáo, who had been serving a suspension after his sending off in the previous round against Fiorentina. Although they trailed by four goals, Setúbal were not going to meekly accept their fate. Instead, they persued the game with vigour. In the 28th minute they finally broke the deadlock when Figueiredo turned Clark on the right goalline and floated over a clever cross that eluded McFaul and landed at the far post, where it was gleefully headed home by Arcanjo.

Tackles came in thick and fast, and Setúbal resorted to some brazen attempts at intimidation, and poor Jim Scott must have been surprised to find himself booked considering the unorthodoxy taking place all around him. Four minutes before half-time United took much of the sting out of the game when Davies scored with a dashing header following a knock-on by Clark from a Foggon corner.

Setúbal huffed and puffed but were not able to breach the Tynesiders' rearguard again until the hour mark. A free-kick temporarily relaxed Newcastle by taking the momentum out of a Setúbal attack and they were stunned when Petita calmly ran up and thumped the ball in from distance. Seven minutes later things got decidedly creaky for Newcastle when Figueiredo scored from a header. At this stage a motorcycle with a huge Vitória Setúbal flag joined the celebrations and began to lap the perimeter wall. If United were going to fold it would be now. This was Joe Harvey's cue to introduce McNamee in place of Burton, and this helped Newcastle to steady the rocking ship.

As the match degenerated into a series of niggling fouls neither side could find any kind of meaningful rhythm, but Newcastle held their nerve and saw out the remainder of the game without further mishap. It was hard not to feel a little sorry for Setúbal, who for a small club had punched well above their weight. Their clash with Newcastle was merely an introduction to playing English sides. In the 1969–70 Fairs Cup they played Liverpool, then in the 1970–71 competition they drew Leeds United, and astonishingly in the 1972–73 tournament they were back in England to face Tottenham Hotspur.

No side beyond the big three of Sporting, Benfica or Porto had won the Portuguese title since Belenenses in 1946, but in consistently getting into the top four and contesting a glut of domestic Cup Finals Setúbal came desperately close. All of which makes Newcastle's triumph over them all the more impressive.

Setúbal Heroes

ERNESTO FIGUEIREDO

Born: Tomar, 6 July 1937.

Career as a player: Sporting Lisbon, Vitória Setúbal.

The Newcastle home programme for the Vitória Setúbal match was unstinting in its praise of Figueiredo and said of him: 'played for Sporting Club Lisbon before joining Setúbal. A tall, rangy player, he is very effective in the air and has scored some vital goals. Although he is nearing the veteran stage at 31, he is playing as well as ever and has three full international caps to his credit.'

En route to facing Newcastle, Setúbal had relied heavily on the goals of Figueiredo. He scored both home and away against Linfield, and another goal in the second round against Lyon and his exquisitely headed goal in the second leg against Newcastle were further evidence of his qualities.

Figueiredo had a good European competiton pedigree. He had been part of the Sporting Lisbon side that won the 1964 Cup-Winners' Cup Final in Brussels, he scored in the first match when Lisbon drew 3–3 with MTK Budapest and was in the replay side that squeezed through 1–0, donning the number-10 jersey for the occasion. He won a total of six caps for Portugal, the first of which came in 1966 against Denmark and the last against England in December 1969.

FERNANDO MASSANO TOMÉ

Born: Setúbal, 1 July 1947.

Career as a player: Vitória Setúbal, Sporting Lisbon.

Career as a coach: Vitória Setúbal 1985–86.

Fernando Massano Tomé.

Between 1985 and 1986 Fernando was the manager of Vitória Setúbal and it is fair to say he was one of the club's favourite sons. This was largely due to his excellent playing record.

Fernando earned a reputation as someone who played well in European competition and he had nine goals at this level. Tomé had a hat-trick in the five-goal demolition of Lyon, so by the time he turned out on Tyneside his fame was growing. An Under-23 and B level international, he was a rising star in the late 1960s. He would return to England in December 1969 to play for Portugal at Wembley, having gained his first cap a few months earlier against Switzerland. He was back in England the following season in the Fairs Cup and gave an impressive display in the heat of Anfield against Liverpool.

JACINTO JOAO

Born: Angola, 25 January 1944.

Career as a player: Benfica, Vitória Setúbal.

In December 1969 Jacinto Joao was in the Portugal side that lost to a Jackie Charlton goal in front of 100,000 England fans at Wembley. He had made a scoring debut just over a year earlier and in netting against Romania gave sight of his exceptional skills. A talented outside-left, he was noted for his speed. During the 1970 World Cup qualifying campaign he was used as a substitute by Portugal to good effect, but he was struggling to impose himself at international level and claimed only 10 caps, which seemed scant reward for such a talented player.

Jacinto Joao.

Joao began his early football career with Benfica, and as a young Angolan living in Portugal struggled to settle. Benfica released him and he joined Setúbal, where away from the glare he developed into a fine player. Nicknamed 'JJ', he scored 66 goals for Setúbal in little over 250 matches. Sadly he was plagued by ill-health later in life and in 2004 he passed away, and such was his reputation at the club that a statue of him was erected on the approach to the ground.

Quarter-Final Results in Full

Leeds United *v.* Újpest Dozsa	0–1	0–2	0–3
Newcastle United *v.* Vitória Setúbal	5–1	1–3	6–4
Rangers *v.* Athletic Bilbao	4–1	0–2	4–3
Göztepe walkover, Hamburger SV withdrew			

Glasgow Rangers

A 'Battle of Britain' in Every Sense

SEMI-FINAL, FIRST LEG

14 May 1969

Rangers 0 **Newcastle United 0**

Rangers: Neef, Johansen, Provan, Greig, Jackson, Smith, Henderson, Penman, Stein, Jardine, Persson.

Newcastle United: McFaul, Craggs, Clark, Gibb, McNamee, Moncur, Scott, Robson, Davies, Arentoft, Foggon.

Subs: Sinclair, Burton, Hope.

Attendance: 75,580

Referee: J. Adair (Belfast)

OFFICIAL SOUVENIR PROGRAMME
PRICE 1/-
INTER CITIES FAIRS' CUP
SEMI-FINAL Second Leg
Season 1968-69
No. 52
NEWCASTLE UNITED
ST. JAMES' PARK - NEWCASTLE UPON TYNE
versus
RANGERS
WEDNESDAY, 21st MAY, 1969
KICK-OFF 7.30 p.m.

A saved penalty by Iam McFaul, a broken nose for Wyn Davies and still Newcastle earned a draw in a packed Ibrox Stadium. This was an example of just how well Newcastle could defend when put to the test. Perhaps the inclusion of four players who had earned a living in the Scottish League provided just the edge that United needed. By now there was a growing sense that United were closing in with some determination on the trophy.

Rangers had vast European experience to call upon and entered the tie as marginal favourites. In 1960 they had reached the European Cup semi-final, and then in 1961 they had reached the Final of the Cup-Winners' Cup. They had repeated the latter feat as recently as 1967 and only playing German opponents in Germany had stood between them and a famous victory. Thus on the Continental stage theirs was a proud and impressive history. They were, in short, a club brought up with and used to success.

Having said that, there was a slightly arrogant side to Rangers which arguably worked against them. To qualify for European football in Scotland had never been too difficult for Rangers or Celtic. The two huge Glasgow sides dominated football north of the border and for all the Edinburgh sides, Dundee or Kilmarnock might annexe the odd Championship, these tended to be but brief moments in the spotlight.

The religious divide that was so marked in Northern Ireland was also visible in Glasgow football. Just as Celtic was recognised as the club of the Roman Catholic half of the west of Scotland and Glasgow, so Rangers were seen as the Protestant club. But while Celtic would sign anyone (and had reaped the rewards in 1967 when winning the European Cup), Rangers had an archaic signing policy which perhaps only Athletic Bilbao in Spain could empathise with. Whereas the Basque club would only sign players born in their local region, Rangers had a policy of not signing Catholics. It was a policy that was increasingly backfiring on the Ibrox club: denied access to some of Scottish football's

The 1968–69 Rangers team.

finest talents they were also attracting among their support an element who were bigoted and insular. In the first leg of the Inter-Cities Fairs Cup Rangers' policy hampered their on-field progress, and in the second leg on Tyneside their policy contributed to a complete breakdown in supporter behaviour.

Although eclipsed at home by Jock Stein's all-conquering Celtic, Rangers were a strong side, studded with internationals. In round one they had eased through against FK Vojvodina of Yugoslavia and in the following tie they thumped little Dundalk of the Irish Republic 9–1 on aggregate. Then, in slightly less convincing fashion, they had beaten DWS of Amsterdam. 'The Basque nation' of Athletic Bilbao failed to halt Rangers in the quarter-finals and so the 'Battle of Britain' tie was set up.

There is no doubt that Rangers were not too impressed with Newcastle's credentials. The Ibrox men viewed United as a moderate English side, incapable of challenging for the English title and long removed from their FA Cup heyday of the 1950s. Newcastle arrived quietly in Glasgow but Joe Harvey was convinced he had a squad that would do the business. He told the assembled Scottish press 'My players know what they have to do. They know it is going to be hard, but they have gathered a lot of experience in a short time and they will go out there and give it everything.'

A party of 16 Newcastle players made the journey over Hadrian's Wall. The travelling party consisted of Gibb, McNamee, Moncur, Scott, Sinclair, McFaul, Hope, Craggs, Craig, Clark, Burton, Elliott, Robson, Davies, Foggon and Arentoft. Wyn 'the Leap' led the United attack despite having played for Wales against England just one week earlier. Also playing in that match had been Ollie Burton, but he did not make the starting team for Ibrox. This may not have been a bad thing, however, as in his place came 'big bad' John McNamee. McNamee had played with Celtic earlier in his career and given the intense rivalry between the two Glasgow clubs he was particularly well versed in anticipating the kind of reception Newcastle could expect. And when he predicted before the game that he would have Rangers' £100,000 striker Colin Stein in his pocket a cheeky marker was placed down.

Wyn Davies was more studied in his comments than McNamee and dispelled the expectation in Glasgow that United would come to defend: 'Remember that our two goals in Zaragoza got us through earlier. So we've got to be on the lookout for an opportunity to score.'

On the eve of the big game United went to the cinema and watched *The Assassination Bureau*, and then on the morning when they were due at Ibrox they trained at Celtic's Parkhead Stadium. The players decided that Jackie Sinclair would be their talisman; after all in six games for Dunfermline Athletic against Rangers he had scored five times. It was he alone who predicted the way the tie would actually go, when he said 'Rangers are always a hard side to beat, particularly at Ibrox Stadium. They are strong physically, too, but I think we can hold them up here and then win at St James' Park.'

Jim Scott also had a good understanding of what made Rangers tick. Although he signed for Newcastle from Edinburgh side Hibernian he was the brother of Alex Scott, who had been something of a golden boy at Rangers. With Tommy Gibb having played for one of Glasgow's other sides, Partick Thistle, there was no shortage of knowledge about the blue half of Glasgow at Newcastle's disposal. Even Joe Harvey's assistant Dave Smith was Scottish, but whereas the players (except big John McNamee) were coy in their comments to the press, Smith was more challenging. When asked how his squad were preparing for the onslaught in Glasgow he upped the ante by saying 'They're all getting ready for Budapest, we've beaten some good sides up until now, so we can beat Rangers.'

There were a few light-hearted moments in the run-up to the tie, however. The *Scottish Daily Express* had Newcastle players and fans alike chuckling when their sports pages decided that the parents of David Craig and John Craggs clearly did not give their lads good enough names. Willie Waddell, then their chief sports writer, announced 'Irish international John Craig is a strong hint for the right-back spot in place of Barry Cragg'. It is not known how David Craig and John Craggs reacted, but for everyone else it was a good giggle.

John Craggs.

As things transpired, the Scottish experience within the squad allied to the confidence gleaned from their good Cup run was highly beneficial to Newcastle. There were over 75,000 inside Ibrox Stadium when the game kicked-off – a record crowd for this competition and discounting FA Cup Finals the biggest attendance Newcastle had ever played in front of. Ibrox Stadium was an impressive ground and one with a long tradition. The Archibald Leitch-inspired main stand was among the finest in the country, and the blue-and-white criss-cross pattern echoed that of the main stand at Newcastle's great rivals Sunderland.

Twelve thousand Newcastle fans journeyed north, and when Irish referee Jack Adam (from the Belfast shipyards no less) got the game underway they made their presence felt with a hearty roar. What would they have felt had they known that one of the linesmen on the night, Mr J.D. Williams of Wrexham, had previously named his house 'Ibrox'!

Oblivious to the apparently partisan nature of the linesman, optimism reigned among the Tyneside travellers. This was partly because Rangers were missing three players who ought to have started. Winger Willie Johnston was suspended and full-back Willie Mathieson had reacted badly to the jabs Rangers' players had taken for a forthcoming trip to Canada. Also missing was the Scotland centre-half Ronnie McKinnon. Although Colin Stein led their attack, he was actually serving a substantial domestic ban such was his short fuse and was therefore low on match practice for the European tie. It was hardly the ideal scenario for the Glasgow club.

Rangers' boss, David White, had predicted a fierce battle before the match. In the run-up to the game he had noted: 'Naturally with the clubs being nearer than is usual in a European competition there will be a big travelling support at both matches. There will be a lot of noise and excitement and we would want it to be well under control.' Perhaps he was predicting what would happen one week later in England but more likely he was priming the referee to watch Newcastle's by now noted physical style. In a barely veiled comment to the referee he noted that he hoped '...for a strictly refereed game

Andy Penman takes the penalty for Rangers.

McFaul dives the right way and pushes the ball round the post.

for I feel that Rangers do better when we get on with the football, like we did when we had a good run earlier in the year.'

As it transpired it was Rangers who were the more aggressive side. The tense mood was highlighted early in the game when young Jardine of Rangers made a dreadful blunder and allowed Davies to gallop unchecked through the centre and straight in on goal. Only a sliced shot saved the home side, and they had an even bigger let-off minutes later when Robson was clean through too. Sadly he elected to try and lob the 'keeper and succeeded only in putting the ball high over the bar.

TOP OF THE CHARTS

Get Back
Beatles and Billy Preston

My Sentimental Friend
Herman's Hermits

Man of the World
Fleetwood Mac

Come Back and Shake Me
Clodagh Rodgers

Goodbye
Mary Hopkin

My Way
Frank Sinatra

Behind a Painted Smile
Isley Brothers

The Israelites
Desmond Decker and the Aces

The Boxer
Simon & Garfunkel

Pinball Wizard
The Who

Rangers recovered from these early scares and soon things were going the Glaswegians' way. Newcastle were penned back for long periods and United rarely threatened; instead they fought a brave rearguard action. The much-awaited clash of the two former Greenock Morton Scandinavians – Johansen of Rangers and United's Arentoft – rarely sparked, and Greig helped subdue Arentoft with a crude tackle for which he was promptly booked.

Ultimately the entire match was best remembered for the penalty save by McFaul. There were 35 minutes gone when Smith slipped a fine pass through the middle and into the path of the flying Swede Orjan Persson. As he headed for goal McFaul rushed off his line and the two collided as the ball broke free. It looked like a 50-50 clash but as Persson slumped to the ground the referee stunned Newcastle and their fans by pointing to the spot. It was a harsh award by any standards and Newcastle, according to the Scottish press, 'protested wildly'.

United had expected Greig to take any penalties, but surprisingly it was Andy Penman, who possessed a blistering shot, who stepped up. When McFaul dived to turn his penalty round the post for a corner the initiative swung the way of the Magpies. Indeed, it was clear that Rangers at this point were a spent force. The robust tackling of McNamee and Moncur increased and Newcastle were barely troubled in the second half.

The Times was in rather more conciliatory mood with the Scots. Their reporter noted that 'Rangers should have had a substantial lead but even missed a penalty'. Perhaps the London correspondent had forgotten the two early chances that United squandered or was objecting to Newcastle's late time-wasting tactics that so riled the Glasgow spectators. He was certainly aggrieved by the string of free-kicks that United conceded in the second half.

The bulk of the Rangers support were disappointed but not despondent. They looked back on a missed penalty and a string of excellent saves by McFaul from Henderson, Jackson, Stein and Penman as evidence that it simply was not their night, but that they were the stronger side.

Joe Harvey, however, summed up the evening's events perfectly. 'We have done this part of the job, now it's up to us to finish it off,' he said after the match. And with that the 'Battle of Britain' headed south over Hadrian's Wall, although, alas, some would take the game's nickname a little too literally.

SEMI-FINAL, SECOND LEG

21 May 1969

Newcastle United 2 **Rangers 0**

Scott 52, Sinclair 77

(Newcastle won 2–0 on aggregate)

Newcastle United: McFaul, Craig, Clark, Gibb, Burton, Moncur, Scott, Robson, Davies, Arentoft, Sinclair.
Subs: Craggs, Foggon, Hope.
Rangers: Neef, Johansen, Mathieson, Greig, McKinnon, Smith, Henderson, Penman, Stein, Johnston, Persson.
Sub: Provan.

Attendance: 59,303
Referee: J. Gough (Swansea)

When the draw for the semi-finals of the Inter-Cities Fairs Cup had been made on 29 March there was immediate interest across Britain. A feisty 'Battle of Britain' was predicted as neither Newcastle or Rangers were known as silky sides and both had a reputation for a no-nonsense approach to football. Rather worryingly, both Tyneside and Clydeside had first-hand experience of the blight of football hooliganism. A number of questions were raised in the aftermath of the draw: who will reach the Final, could the Cup be staying in Britain, will the tie pass without incident?

Newcastle deputy chief constable Jack Marshall was quick to reassure the public that his force could handle the inevitably tense second leg. 'We have dealt with Glasgow crowds before. We take steps to deal with football crowds as we do anything else,' he reassured everyone. 'It will involve extra men but if Newcastle United look after their side of it we will do our damndest to look after our side of it.'

Perhaps it was just coincidence, but United did away with their black, white and green programme cover for the tie. Instead they issued a special programme where the cover was halved vertically, one side given over to black and white and the other rendered in Rangers' colours of blue and white. Tickets were scarce. To stand on the terracing had required a brief

The police move in to clear the pitch of Rangers' fans.

that had cost 7/6, and by the afternoon of the game these were changing hands for £1. Centre stand tickets valued at £2 were available from touts at a staggering £8.

For those who were not there, the following morning's headlines were stunning. For once sensationalism was entirely appropriate and few sub-editors could actually over-exaggerate as the news began to filter in of the mayhem that unfolded in and around St James' Park.

Once the pitch was cleared the wounded could be seen to.

'Rioting, battling Rangers fans surged onto the pitch at St James' Park, Newcastle, last night amid a maelstrom of bottles and glasses in an apparent bid to halt their team's Fairs City Cup semi-final with Newcastle United.' So ran the opening paragraph on the front page of the early editions of the *Scottish Daily Express*; and this topic was typical across the range of papers.

'At the end of a violent, sickening evening Newcastle had eased into the Fairs Cup Final, but that wasn't the immediate talking point. United had progressed but only after drunken Scottish hooligans threatened to end the night prematurely. How ironic that it should be two Scots in the United team who scored the decisive goals.'

It is interesting to see how the world beyond the Gallowgate viewed the nights events. *The Scotsman* pulled no punches. In a stinging opening paragraph its front page screamed in bold type:

'Newcastle was under siege last night as violence erupted in all quarters of the city. Mobs of Rangers supporters, their team defeated 2–0, smashed their way through the streets. Police, ambulances and hospitals were swamped with calls for help. More than 100 people have been injured in a stadium melee.'

Strong stuff but sadly accurate.

To concentrate on the run-up to the game itself is useful before the carnage of the evening itself is explored. For those who think that mind-games and managerial jousting are new things and the preserve of Sir Alex Ferguson or Jose Mourinho then think again. Such shenanigans were alive and well in 1969!

The build-up to the game was interesting. Newcastle had not lost at home since early October and were thus fully justified in being confident. Manager Joe Harvey was quite open in his optimism: 'I'm not worried about the outcome,' he quite frankly told inquisitive pressmen.

The Scotsman newspaper suggested that Newcastle were being over-confident and even said that 'Newcastle's approach is bordering on the cocky'. But United had already beaten Celtic twice in that season, and Celtic had taken both the League and Scottish Cup from under the Ibrox club's nose. There was good reason for Newcastle United to be bold and brash in their assessment of the game – they had survived the Rangers onslaught in Glasgow without too much difficulty.

Willie Waddell was a football writer on *The Express* staff and a former Rangers legend. Indeed, he was one of the finest post-war players to come out of Scotland. He would later manage Rangers with major success and he was in every sense a footballing giant north of the border. He was in no doubt that Rangers, with their rich European tradition, would sweep aside United on Tyneside. 'A Rangers victory is on the cards. Surely they can beat a team that includes Tommy Gibb, Preben Arentoft, Jim Scott and Jackie Sinclair, who were only ordinary players in Scotland before they moved south.' It was a delicate little barb, but as the leading newspaper in Scotland at the time it was a significant dig at Newcastle United and the quality of their staff. It was also by no means untypical of the sentiments north of the border. Yet while Rangers were able to welcome back the dangerous Willie Johnston as well as defenders Ronnie McKinnon and Willie Mathieson, there would be one key omission in the Newcastle team. Former Celtic defender John McNamee would be out, still hampered by a thigh strain he had picked up in Glasgow. The way he had contained Scotland centre-forward Colin Stein in Glasgow had been crucial to United's success.

Rangers' fans swarmed into Newcastle for the tie, such is the proximity of Tyneside from Clydeside. Unfortunately, before, during and after the game their loutish behaviour soured what should have been a thrilling evening. Several Newcastle fans were set upon as they made their way to the ground, and a threatening atmosphere filled the city.

Having said that, it would be churlish to ignore that St James' Park had witnessed serious football hooliganism earlier in the season when the visit of Manchester City on FA Cup duty saw fighting on the terracing and in the streets, during which the police made several arrests. More ominously, in February 1968 a visit from Celtic for a friendly was also marred by trouble.

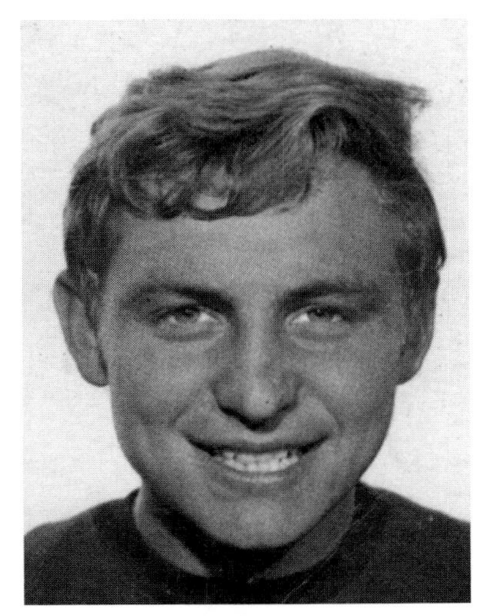

Neef, the Rangers 'keeper.

Trouble was evident from mid-afternoon as excessive drinking took its toll. Journalists walking from Central Station to the ground noted the loutish behaviour that was already present. When a gate was broken down at the Gallowgate End (where the Rangers support congregated) before the game the mood was set.

The tone of the game did little to defuse the powder-keg atmosphere. This was a hard, mean game which neither side could look back on with

Scott scored Newcastle's first goal.

Sinclair fires in the second for Newcastle.

pride. Against a menacing backdrop the game lacked any rhythm or style. On the quarter-hour mark Neef saved from a close-in Robson shot and soon afterwards McKinnon tested McFaul in the home goal.

The first hint of the troubles to come in the stadium came when Davies and McKinnon clashed on the stroke of half-time. Punches were traded as players engaged in an unseemly melee. At this the Rangers end erupted, fans swarmed over the touchline and missiles were thrown onto the pitch, several of them aimed at United players.

Jackie Sinclair.

In the 53rd minute of a match with few chances Newcastle scored when Scott ran in from an angle, following a mis-placed pass by McKinnon, and drove a shot beyond Neef into the far corner of the net. This triggered a second pitch invasion – but this time it was a rather more good natured affair led by exuberant Tyneside youngsters, which was a common

Bobby Moncur heads clear from two Rangers players.

occurrence at football grounds at that time and had none of the menace of hooliganism attached.

McKinnon was injured soon after the goal and Provan replaced him, but it did nothing to blunt the United assault and the game still flowed the way of the Rangers goal. When Davies nodded a delightful pass into the path of Sinclair, the lithe Scot drilled the final nail into Rangers' coffin. It was no more than Newcastle deserved as they were marginally the better of two underperforming sides.

Sinclair's goal brought hordes of Rangers fans onto the pitch clearly intent on achieving an abandonment of the match. For 17 minutes large numbers of police with Alsatian dogs battled to restore order. They eventually did so and the match was able to conclude, but the atmosphere was dreadful and the match finished with both sides merely going through the motions. So Newcastle, from being perennial cup 'also rans' made it to the Final, but they did so on a night that will be remembered on Tyneside for all the wrong reasons.

United director William McKeag called the scenes the worst he had seen in 50 years of watching football. John Gibson in the *Newcastle Chronicle* perhaps best captured the mood, calling this 'The night soccer wept for the name of Glasgow Rangers'.

Rangers captain John Greig (who would be denied a chance to hold aloft the European Cup-Winners' Cup due to fan misbehaviour in Barcelona in 1972) was embarrassed and told waiting pressmen that 'We, the players, feel disgusted with the fans who caused the trouble'.

Joe Harvey appeared bemused: 'It beats me how Rangers could play so well with a support like that behind them.' All in all, it had been a scrappy game, an ill–tempered joust that ended up being, as one pressman put it, 'a sorry parody of what a European glamour tie should be.'

The cleaning-up operation began almost immediately after the end of the game as the supporters drifted away, but Newcastle remained a city with an atmosphere and violent undercurrent for some hours. From the Gallowgate down to the railway station numerous incidents occurred. *The Express* noted that 'Police in groups of six stood on corners as the Rangers fans made their way back to the railway station and a special coach park. All coaches were warned to be out of Newcastle by 11.00pm. A squad of 100 police with dogs ringed Manor Station as three special trains packed with Rangers supporters left the city.'

BATTLE OF BRITAIN

The meeting of Newcastle and Rangers was not the first all-British clash in European competition by any means. But it has to be said that when these clashes had involved Rangers playing away from home there had been a catalogue of incidents. It is notable in the list of clashes below that the only other match that attracted headlines for the wrong reasons was Celtic's visit to Merseyside when a disputed goal provoked trouble on the terraces.

1960–61

Cup-Winners' Cup

Rangers 2 Wolves 0 & Wolves 1 RANGERS 1

1962–63

Cup-Winners' Cup

Tottenham 5 Rangers 2 & Rangers 2 TOTTENHAM 3

Fairs Cup

Everton 1 Dunfermline 0 & DUNFERMLINE 2 Everton 0

1963–64

Cup-Winners' Cup

Tottenham 2 Manchester Utd 0 & MANCHESTER UTD 4 Tottenham 1

1964–65

Fairs Cup

Kilmarnock 0 Everton 2 & EVERTON 4 Kilmarnock 1

1965–66

Cup-Winners' Cup

Celtic 1 Liverpool 0 & LIVERPOOL 2 Celtic 0

1966–67

Fairs Cup

Leeds 4 Kilmarnock 2 & Kilmarnock 0 LEEDS 0

1967–68

Fairs Cup

Leeds 1 Hibernian 0 & Hibernian 1 LEEDS 1

Rangers 0 Leeds 0 & LEEDS 2 Rangers 0

Dundee 1 Leeds 1 & LEEDS 1 Dundee 0

1968–69

Cup-Winners' Cup

Dunfermline 0 West Brom 0 & West Brom 0 DUNFERMLINE 1

Fairs Cup

Chelsea 5 Morton 0 & Morton 3 CHELSEA 4

Rangers 0 Newcastle 0 & NEWCASTLE 2 Rangers 0

Back in Glasgow the locals by and large were horrified by what had unfolded. At Glasgow Central Railway Station half a dozen policemen with dogs awaited the return of the special trains that brought many of the Rangers supporters home. Taxi ranks were deserted with the Glasgow Taxi Owners' Association warning their drivers to stay clear of Central Station.

Meanwhile, the Fairs Cup Committee were already planning an inquiry. Sir Stanley Rous was the chairman of the group and he was immediately appointed as the man who would sit in judgement on the evening's events.

It was quickly established that Harry Cavan would be asked for his observations (he had been FIFA's observer) and that the referee would also be asked for his views on what had happened. With UEFA only looking after the European Cup and Cup-Winners' Cup at that time the Fairs Cup would ask its own general assembly to decide on what, if any, punishment was appropriate, and their secretary Pieter Joris would have a key role to play. Remarkably, looking back on events now it seems incredible that Rangers escaped with only a firm warning.

So what had sparked the rioting? The answer is probably a complex combination of factors – the sheer volume of visiting supporters and the easy access they had to drink, the disappointment of a dreadfully disappointing end to Rangers' season and an ill-advised tannoy announcement which had made an abandonment seem possible. Brian Glanville noted at the time in his *World Football Handbook* that some of the Rangers supporters were chanting 'We Want Trouble' and that this was not the first example of Glaswegian hooliganism in the North East. Rangers clearly had an issue with the behaviour of some of their fans, but the vast bulk of Glasgow football fans were appalled by the scenes they had witnessed; one, the local Church of Scotland minister in Ibrox, even went as far as handing back his free season ticket, while the club chairman, John Lawrence, acknowledged that the club had a historical legacy to tackle.

Finally thoughts could turn to the other semi-final. Without doubt it had been a much more one-sided affair and Újpest Dozsa had, as expected, sailed through with room to spare. The results over the two legs were:

Göztepe Izmir 1 (Gaglayan (pen)), Újpest Dozsa 4 (Bene 2, A Dunai 2)
Újpest Dozsa 4 (Bene 3, Nagy), Göztepe Izmir 0

Having reached the semi-final by dint of Hamburger SV (their quarter-final opponents) withdrawing from the competition, the Turkish side Göztepe Izmir were still a bit of an unknown quantity. Although now a Third Division side, there was a time when Göztepe were one of the best supported clubs in Turkey. It mattered little, for they were no match for the fine Hungarian side. Bene confirmed his status as one of Europe's finest players by lashing home no fewer than five goals over the two ties. Antal Dunai, who had scored the goal that beat Leeds at Elland Road in the quarter-finals, also grabbed a brace in the first leg.

Scottish Stars

JOHN GREIG MBE

Born: Edinburgh, 11 September 1942.
Career as a player: Rangers (1961–78).
Career as a manager: Rangers (1978–83).

Arguably 'Mr Rangers', Greig was an inspirational wing-half who captained Rangers for many years and was a veteran of the European stage, playing in three Cup-Winners' Cup Finals and, of course, the Fairs Cup semi-final in 1969. He played in over 800 matches for Rangers, an astonishing total in the modern era, and won 44 Scotland caps. Rangers granted him a well earned testimonial in 1978 and over 65,000 attended.

John Greig.

Greig was the epitome of a one-club man and managed Rangers for five years before drifting into the public relations side of the club. On three occasions he played in Rangers sides that won the 'treble', yet much of his career was destined to be spent in the shadow of Jock Stein's all-conquering Celtic side of the late 1960s and early 1970s. Interestingly, in March 1966 Greig had starred in the Scottish League side that beat their English counterparts 3–1 at St James' Park.

There remains debate about why he did not take the penalty-kick that Rangers earned against Newcastle at Ibrox in the first leg of the semi-final. He had taken one earlier in the tournament and Newcastle certainly expected him – and not Andy Penman – to step up to the penalty spot. Of course, Penman saw his kick blocked and the save by McFaul proved crucial in the overall outcome of the tie.

WILLIE JOHNSTON

Born: Glasgow, 19 December 1946.
Career as a player: Lochare Welfare, Rangers (1964–72), West Bromwich Albion (1972–79), Vancouver Whitecaps (1979–80), Birmingham City (1979–80), Rangers (1980–82), Vancouver Whitecaps, Hearts (1982–84), East Fife (1984–85).

Willie Johnston.

Willie Johnston earned a degree of notoriety in the world of football when he sensationally failed a drugs test while representing Scotland in the 1978 World Cup Finals in Argentina. A flying left-winger, Johnston was a fixture at Rangers for many years and in earning 22 Scotland caps he served vivid notice of his abilities. It was deemed good fortune on the part of Newcastle that Johnston was not available for the first-leg clash at Ibrox. He had played in the 1967 Cup-Winners' Cup Final and scored when Rangers won that tournament in 1972. Johnston had a dreadful disciplinary record – he was sent off 16 times in his career but was rather subdued when he played at St James' Park, where he got little change out of David Craig and increasingly played at inside-left.

COLIN STEIN

Born: Linlithgow, 10 May 1947.

Career as a player: Armadale Thistle, Hibernian (1965–68), Rangers (1968–72), Coventry City (1972–75), Rangers (1975–78), Kilmarnock (1977–78).

Colin Stein.

A Scotland centre-forward of some note, Stein spent some time in England when he joined Coventry City. He sprang to national fame in October 1968 when Hibernian sold their then star striker to Rangers for £100,000 – the first-ever six-figure transfer between Scottish clubs. Ironically, around this time the media had linked Newcastle with Stein, this on the back of a poor run from Wyn Davies.

Stein accumulated 21 Scotland caps and even scored four in one match against Cyprus in May 1969. Against Newcastle in the Fairs Cup Burton and McNamee held him in check and probably benefitted from the fact that Stein was serving a domestic ban that meant he could only play in international and European fixtures at the time of the semi-final clash. But Stein's European ambitions were fulfilled in due course and in 1972 he scored twice in the European Cup-Winners' Cup Final when Rangers beat Dynamo Moscow in Barcelona. It was a pity for his overall progress that rather like Willie Johnston he had a sharp temper and was not unknown to referees.

Újpest Dozsa

Captain Bobby Wins the Day…Twice!

FINAL, FIRST LEG

29 May 1969

Newcastle United 3 **Újpest Dozsa 0**

Moncur 63, 72, Scott 83

Newcastle: McFaul, Craig, Clark, Gibb, Burton, Moncur, Scott, Robson, Davies, Arentoft, Sinclair.

Sub: Foggon, Hope, Craggs.

Újpest: Szentmihályi, Káposzta, Solymosi, Bankuti, Nosko, E. Dunai, Göröcs, Fazekas, Bene, A. Dunai, Zámbó.

Subs: Szini, Nyiro, Nagy.

Attendance: 59,234

Referee: Joseph Hannet (Belgium)

OFFICIAL SOUVENIR PROGRAMME
PRICE
1/-
INTER CITIES
FAIRS' CUP
FINAL TIE
First Leg
Season 1968-69
No. 53
NEWCASTLE
UNITED
ST. JAMES' PARK - NEWCASTLE UPON TYNE
versus
UJPEST DOZSA
THURSDAY, 29th MAY, 1969
KICK-OFF 7.30 p.m.

Barely a week after the Rangers match St James's Park was full once more. If Newcastle United were to win the Fairs Cup then they would have to beat the conquerors of Cup holders and favourites Leeds United. This was the single most important fact that concerned sports writers in England during the run-up to the Final. Leeds United may not have been loved across England but they were universally respected. Don Revie's Yorkshire side was full of grit and had established a new First Division record when they landed the title – not a single English side had been able to beat them at Elland Road and they had lost just two games in the entire gruelling League campaign. In winning at Leeds, Újpest had perhaps put down a great psychological marker. At any rate, it certainly vexed the English press.

Újpest Dozsa were undeniably one of Hungary's finest sides and boasted a number of players who had played for Hungary in the 1966 World Cup Finals. The bookmakers agreed that they were an impressive

The Újpest Dozsa team.

club and that Newcastle faced a tall order, indeed the bookies were crystal clear in how they thought things would go; Újpest were 2/1 on to win the Cup. The chances for Britain's sole European Final representatives were not looking too rosy.

Újpest had in their ranks the two leading marksmen in the competition. On the way to reaching the Final Antal Dunai had scored 10 goals for Újpest and his teammate Ferenc Bene had chipped in with nine. And this was a strike-force with vast experience of the big stage. But their coach, Lajos Baróti, knew that coming to Tyneside would mean a rearguard action for the bulk of the game. 'We think Newcastle are rather like Leeds. Their style is quite similar but there are dangers,' he told the press at Newcastle Airport. He then concluded by noting that he '...became aware of these dangers when I watched them against Rangers last week here. I gathered great respect for Wyn Davies and noticed the rest of the team puts a lot of long high balls to his head. I was also impressed by your wingers Scott and Sinclair, who are fast and took their goals well.'

It was not surprising that Baróti had been impressed at St James'. There was no doubt that United were in quite excellent form at home. Only two sides had won at St James' Park all season and one of those was Championship winners Leeds United. So, if Újpest were to beat Newcastle they would have to negotiate a raucous and turbulent night on Tyneside, and no doubt the maulings that Rangers, Feyenoord and Setúbal had taken would have been in the back of Baróti's mind.

Joe Harvey recognised that the first leg could be decisive, and on the evening of the match he was quite open about his ambitions for the Tyneside leg: 'Nobody comes to St James' and gets away with it. Our lads can rise to the occasion with this great crowd of supporters behind them.' He then dropped something of a bombshell when he added 'It would have been nice if I'd been able to have seen Újpest myself and been more settled in my mind. But let them worry about us over here and not us them.'

Bobby Moncur.

Of course, it was not that Harvey had been lax in not seeing Újpest. Quite simply the way the season had ended in a fixture log jam had conspired against him. Rightly his focus had remained on his own team and getting the job at hand done, rather than looking too far in advance. Harvey was a solid man-manager and he was also a very pragmatic man who knew his mind and tackled tasks in a studied order. But when big games come calling managers have to devolve a huge amount of responsibility to the men who take the field. Truly great players become big figures in special matches and so it proved here. The man of the moment turned out to be Newcastle skipper Bobby Moncur.

Before the match Bobby noted with some modesty that 'I will never be a crowd puller. I am an average player who has made the grade through dedication.' If that was the case then Bobby was about to reap his rewards. There were certainly bigger names on the field that evening but nobody outshone Moncur.

The day of the match dragged across Tyneside. Schoolboys were distracted, workers clock-watched and an almost tangible tension swept across the city. Finally the afternoon gave way to evening and all roads led to St James' Park. A crowd of 59,234 paid record receipts of £42,150, and had the weather been kinder the ground would have been even fuller. Time has dimmed the memory of many but John Andrews of Gateshead was the one person I spoke to who recalled that ticket touts had to give

Bobby Moncur (not shown) scores Newcastle's first goal.

away tickets in the run-up to the Újpest Dozsa match at St James'. Wet weather saw 10s tickets (which had been going for £2 10s and £3) plunge in value as the weather worsened. The sodden touts eventually cut their losses to the point where they were even seen to hand out tickets as they trudged away from the stadium.

The first half, it has been widely agreed, was a tetchy affair with neither side able to settle to any real pattern. There was a lot of hustle and bustle but the quality players could not get time on the ball, and there was a hesitancy and tension among the players that led to the ball being in constant motion and no time being given to any of the potential match winners. Tackles were firm but generally fair, although Solymosi was booked for a rash lunge on Robson that swept the diminutive striker's feet away from him.

Thankfully, the second half was much more of a spectacle. Three minutes after the hour a finely placed Gibb free-kick was floated over and found Wyn Davies in space. The Welsh striker chested the ball down, ran on and forced a shot towards the Hungarian 'keeper. The ball ran loose and unexpectedly the first man to the free ball was none other than captain Bobby Moncur. He may have been without a goal all season but he made light of the awkward height of the ball to volley a shot into the far corner of the net.

Tyneside erupted. At this stage no one in the grand old stadium could predict how the match would end but one thing was for sure – Newcastle now had a chance of taking a lead to Budapest. In an instant some of the tension disappeared. Newcastle at last had something to build on, Újpest on the other hand had a decision to make. Should they change tack and try to snatch an away goal or should they remain content that they could claw back a one-goal deficit back in Hungary?

Sinclair on the left was beginning to look lame, an earlier knock had begun to impact on his mobility and Joe Harvey had to withdaw him. In his place he sent on teenage winger Alan Foggon. But the change did not impact on the flow of the game, Newcastle now had the bit between their teeth and were pursuing a second goal. And in the 72nd minute it duly arrived.

Sensationally, it was Moncur again who scored. Nine minutes after his opening goal Moncur played a skilful one-two with Preben Arentoft. The Dane often delighted the Geordie fans, and his return pass set Moncur straight through the centre of the Újpest defence, and when the ball sat up nicely the captain was able to slam another goal past the outstanding Szentmihályi. It was an unlikely double for Bobby Moncur but a vital one for United. The difference between defending a two-goal lead in Eastern Europe and a one-goal lead was going to be huge.

But United would not be defending a two-goal lead.

Arentoft was by now making a real impact on the game and he set up a remarkable third goal. This time he slipped a great pass to Scott, and the winger called upon all of his European experience to stretch out a toe and lift the ball over the advancing 'keeper for a third. Eighty-three minutes gone under the Tyneside floodlights and United had one hand on the trophy. It finished 3–0 to Newcastle.

In the aftermath of the match, however, it was important that Newcastle did not get carried away. There had been several great European fightbacks in the past, many of which involved British sides. In the 1961–62 European Cup Spurs had lost 4–2 in Zabrze only to win 8–1 at White Hart Lane. The other side of the coin was that Manchester United had beaten Sporting Lisbon 4–1 at Old Trafford only to lose 5–0 in Lisbon. The message was clear…take nothing for granted.

FINAL, SECOND LEG

11 June 1969

Újpest Dozsa 2	**Newcastle United 3**
Bene 31, Göröcs 44	*Moncur 46, Arentoft 50, Foggon 70*

(Newcastle won Cup 6–2 on aggregate)

Újpest Dozsa: Szentmihályi, Káposzta, Solymosi, Nosko, Bankuti, E. Dunai, Göröcs, Fazekas, Bene, A. Dunai, Zámbó.
Newcastle: McFaul, Craig, Clark, Gibb, Burton, Moncur, Scott, Robson, Davies, Arentoft, Sinclair.
Sub: Foggon.

Attendance: 34,000
Referee: Joseph Heymann (Switzerland)

And so to the second leg and United's date with destiny. However, although the match engrossed Tyneside and Budapest it was overshadowed by events both internationally and nationally as 1969 lurched from crisis to crisis. American President Richard Nixon was agonising over whether to withdraw from the bloody morass of the Vietnam war, while Enoch Powell had made a speech in England that had thrust immigration into the political spotlight in dramatic fashion. Prime Minister Harold Wilson was at loggerheads with the Trades Unions and in

TOP OF THE CHARTS

The Ballad of John and Yoko
The Beatles
Dizzy
Tommy Roe
Oh Happy Days
Edwin Hawkins Singers
Man of the World
Fleetwood Mac
Get Back
Beatles with Billy Preston
Time is Tight
Booker T and the MGs
My Way
Frank Sinatra
The Boxer
Simon & Garfunkel
The Tracks of My Tears
Smokey Robinson and The Miracles
Ragamuffin Man
Manfred Mann

short there was very little good news to cheer.

Thus it was against this backdrop in what was more a cricket month than a traditional football month that Newcastle sought to bring a little sunshine to Tyneside on the sporting front. Fifteen minutes before Newcastle's party landed in Hungary the Hungarian national side flew in from their World Cup qualifier in Eire. They had beaten the Republic of Ireland 2–1 in Dublin and Újpest players Szentmihályi, Káposzta, Zámbó, Bene, Göröcs and Dunai were all part of the team which had won a key qualifier.

When United's flight touched down in Budapest they were met by a gaggle of pressmen. Joe Harvey was considered in what he said and set exactly the right tone when he conceded that: 'It will still be difficult despite our three-goal lead. But I would like to take the Cup back to Newcastle and I hope to play a full strength side.' Of course, the great unspoken truth was that throughout their marathon run to the Final United had not won a single match away from home.

The Newcastle squad found it hard to relax before such a big game. The players were sent on a cruise down the Danube but little could take their mind off the growing suspicion that Újpest had been below par on Tyneside and would come roaring out the blocks in Budapest.

The second leg in Budapest could hardly have been a greater contrast to the first. Newcastle endured a torrid opening 45 minutes and reached the safety of the interval nursing a two-goal deficit and looking to all intents and purposes as if they were going to let European glory slip from their grasp. However, on a near perfect pitch a night of wonderful football theatre unfolded. The black-and-white diagonally painted goal-frames only added a touch of the exotic to what was already an intoxicating evening. Several thousand Newcastle fans made it to the game, others made do with what turned out to be very brief but very enjoyable BBC highlights back home. It goes without saying that these were black-and-white excerpts. Indeed, a look back on the evening's entertainment offered by the BBC shows how life has changed since 1969. At 7.30pm *It's a Knockout* took centre stage, then *Wink To Me Only* occupied half an hour before a 15-minute news bulletin. United fans then had to try to concentrate on *The Wednesday Play* with Leo McKern, before finally at 11.00pm the highlights from Budapest were screened. If that list of offerings was not up to scratch the main alternative was through Tyne Tees, where *The Saint* was the highlight of the evening. The contrast between this approach in the days of only two major channels and the wall-to-wall football coverage of today's situation, where there are multiple channels, is amazing.

Kitted out in all-white, Újpest looked and played rather like Real Madrid, and indeed in the first half something of a white blizzard descended upon the United goal. Újpest's opening goal in the 31st minute came after a period of sustained pressure and was netted by one of their world-class players, Bene. The move started innocuously enough in their own half with a series of neat, square passes. Bene picked the ball up half-way inside the Newcastle half, skipped past Arentoft and released the ball to Antal Dunai. In typical Bene fashion he continued his run into the

United penalty area, and when Dunai prodded the ball forward there was a half chance for Fazekas before the ball broke to Bene, who was by now at a tight angle to the goal and seemingly posing only minimal threat. But with the skill and drive that had made him a genuine international star he thumped an incredible low drive into the bottom of the net, beating McFaul with greater ease than might have been expected.

The second Újpest goal started from a throw-in to the Hungarians deep inside the right side of their own half. The ball was tossed forward to Bene, who was tackled by Moncur and dispossesed only for Sinclair to lose the ball immediately on the half-way line. Quick as a flash E. Dunai picked up the loose ball and with the outside of his boot found Göröcs in acres of room on the left. Göröcs sped forward, went between two defenders and as McFaul came out to narrow the angle the forward simply blasted it low into the net at the near post. Coming as it did in the 44th minute it seemed to not only put a full-stop on a depressing first half for United but was arguably a portent of what was to come in the second half. United were crestfallen and visibly shaken by the pounding they had taken in that opening 45 minutes.

As the *Daily Express* succinctly put it. 'The half-time whistle came as a great relief to Newcastle, who were penned back in defence. Indeed, had the Hungarians got the goals they deserved, and they ones they should never have missed, they would have more than wiped out Newcastle's lead in the first half.'

However, a half-time talk by manager Joe Harvey (celebrating his 51st birthday) turned things around. He apparently told his players to 'get a goal and they will fold like a concertina'. Stories vary as to Harvey's exact words on the night. Full-back David Craig recalls Harvey saying 'I haven't a clue how you are going to get a goal, and I don't much care, but score one you can. And you will. After that our troubles will be over and Újpest will fold.' Harvey was right and just 60 seconds into the second half captain courageous Bobby Moncur stepped forward to ease the tension.

The goal that made United's night came from a corner by Jackie Sinclair. His initial kick was cleared, but only straight back to him. When he returned it with greater accuracy Moncur was there to crash it into the roof of the Újpest net. The sense of deflation experienced by the Hungarians is hard to capture. It simply seemed that all of the first-half dominance and good work was undone in an instant. The initiative was gone, and worse still Newcastle now had a precious away goal. Visibly rattled, arguably Újpest never really regained the upper hand in the tie.

Moncur's opener was certainly a signal for a glorious four-minute spell in which United scored again and killed the tie. The goal that did the business for Newcastle was a strange one. From the Újpest goalkeeper the ball floated into the Newcastle half and Moncur simply thumped it straight back to the right-back position in the Újpest half. Unfortunately for Újpest their right-back, Káoszta, slipped instead of cooly dealing with the long-ball. Sinclair quickly pounced on the loose ball and floated over a deep cross, which although headed clear by Újpest fell kindly to Jim Scott. The little winger jinked cleverly and unleashed a powerful left-foot shot from the edge of the area – and here Lady Luck took a shine to Newcastle. The ball ricocheted off an Újpest defender who was sliding in desperately, looped up into the air and fell near the penalty spot, where Preben Arentoft was in splendid

Newcastle players wheel away in celebration.

Iam McFaul beats the ball away to keep the scores level.

isolation. He needed no invitation to thrash a left-foot volley on the drop over the 'keeper's head into the roof of the Újpest net near the junction of post and bar. In truth it was an unsavable shot.

Suddenly, from a situation of near desperation at half-time the match stood at 2–2 on the night and United were amazingly in easy street with a 5–2 aggregate lead. Lajos Baróti's side were shattered and it was clear the Cup would be going to England.

However, United pushed on for another goal and when Alan Foggon replaced Jim Scott they introduced the evening's match winner. From a long McFaul goal-kick the ball was headed on by Wyn Davies, and when it landed between two defenders it allowed Foggon to burst clear and score the winning goal in the 70th minute. For a youngster of only 19 the goal spoke volumes not only for his speed and composure but also for his potential (he was already an England Youth international). He carried the ball at pace beyond defenders before lashing in a shot which the 'keeper could only turn onto the bar and Foggon was first to react to ram the loose ball home from just inches out.

Jim Scott scores at the Gallowgate end in the first leg.

The presentation of the Cup was informal but dramatic. Made on the pitch itself a scrum of photographers, reporters and local worthies milled around but parted to allow Bobby Moncur to walk up to the dignitaries who presented the trophy from a table top. He quickly raised the Cup to the stand behind the officials and then the trophy was passed on to Iam McFaul. McFaul, Sinclair, Davies, Arentoft…they all trooped along behind Moncur and in sharp contrast to today's podium-shaking dances they merely gave a manly handshake before making their way back to join captain Moncur. A lovely 'join in if you want' lap of honour followed with a gaggle of fans in attendance and the vast bulk of the Hungarian crowd staying back to applaud United.

Praise for Newcastle was quick to come. *The Times* in London hailed this as 'a victory in style, a 6–2 destruction of the Hungarian League leaders was no mean feat. The two-goal blitz in the four minutes or so after the interval had done the trick.'

Joe Harvey was ecstatic: 'I have not seen any Cup Final or played in one that matched this game for excitement and fighting courage,' he told the

English sports writers who were with him after the game. 'It was a remarkable performance by any standard to beat Újpest on their own ground. I'm terribly proud of my boys and I know the whole city of Newcastle will be thrilled. We began as outsiders in the Fairs Cup and finished real champions.'

Brian Glanville, the greatest football writer of his generation, captured the scale of Newcastle's achievement superbly: 'To thrash the powerful Újpest 3–0 in the first leg of the Final, after the Hungarians had beaten Leeds so categorically, was a fine achievement. To beat them again in Budapest was staggering.'

Spare a thought, though, for Hungarian football. So often an elegant bridesmaid, they had seen Ferencváros lose the 1968 Inter-Cities Fairs Cup Final in Budapest to Leeds United and now almost one year on the same fate had now befallen their other great club Újpest Dozsa.

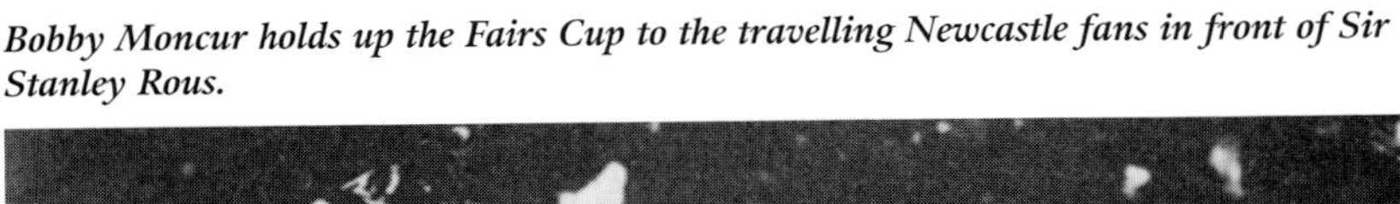

Bobby Moncur holds up the Fairs Cup to the travelling Newcastle fans in front of Sir Stanley Rous.

As United trooped off to celebrate there was a full-stop to the evening's triumph. In Switzerland the footballing authorities had decided that the Inter-Cities Fairs Cup was to be renamed in the near future, but that had not stopped them making the draw for the following year's competition in which the holders would play Dundee United. 'The Holders'...now that had a certain ring to it that sounded good!

Hungarian Heroes

FERENC BENE

Born: Balatonújlak, 17 December 1944.
Career as a player: Újpest Dozsa (1961–78), Volán FC (1978–79 & 1983–84), Sepsi-78 (1981–82), Soroksári Vose (1984), Kecskeméti SC (1985).

A Hungarian international who gathered 76 caps, Ferenc Bene was one of the great footballers of his era. Hugely dangerous around the penalty area, his finishing was clinical, and although he exuded energy he could retain his composure in front of goal with alarming iciness. His goal against Brazil in the 1966 World Cup was one of the all-time great international strikes and he netted in each and every one of Hungary's four games in England.

With Újpest regular European contestants his experience grew rapidly, and when he added vast international experience he became a most accomplished opponent. In all Bene scored 36 goals in 76 internationals, making his debut against the then Yugoslavia in 1962 and ending his international career in 1976 against Czechoslovakia. However, it was as a member of the famous lilac-and-white-clad Újpest Dozsa that he

Ferenc Bene.

really made his biggest impression. Signed as a 17-year-old in 1961, Bene sprung to prominence with them and then made a mark on the world stage in the 1964 Olympics when he scored six in one match against Morocco and 12 in the tournament overall. Five times he was the top scorer in Hungarian seasons and in 1962 he grabbed six goals in one League match. Yet for all his prowess in front of goal he was unlucky in that he served Újpest initially in a period when they struggled to land the League title. They finally did so in 1969 but only by a single point from their great rivals Ferencváros. This was a Championship win that broke the flood barriers and Újpest enjoyed a period of domination thereafter. It was this spell of belated success that finally helped Bene amass his eight Championship medals.

He spent the twilight of his career in Finland but returned to Budapest to coach and at one time was national coach to the Hungarian ladies' side. Sadly, he died at the relatively young age of 61 in 2006 following a fall near his home.

ANTAL DUNAI

Born: Gara, 21 March 1943.
Career as a player: Pécsi Dozsa, Újpest Dozsa (1965–1977), Debreceni VSC.
Career as a manager: Real Betis, CD Castellón, Zalaegerszegi TE, Real Murcia, Levante UD, Veszprémi LC, Debreceni VSC.

Antal Dunai.

Also known as Dunai II, Antal was with Újpest between 1965 and 1977 and was a noted marksman throughout that time. He, like his teammate Ferenc Bene, was also a quality international and scored nine goals in 31 appearances for Hungary, having served notice of his abilities in winning an Olympic Gold Medal in the victorious Hungarian side of 1964. He was Europe's top scorer in 1967 and second top scorer in 1968. From 1967 onwards the revered French football magazine *France Football* awarded a golden boot to the top scorer in European Leagues. In 1968 with 36 goals it was only the remarkably gifted Eusebio of Benfica who edged out Antal, and one year later with 31 goals Antal finished third in this 'unofficial' competition. Back home in Hungary he topped the scoring charts in 1967, 1968 and 1970 with 36, 31 and 14 League goals respectively.

In common with many of his teammates he had a flair for coaching and gave notable service to a number of sides, including four in Spain's La Liga.

JÁNOS GÖRÖCS

Born: Gánt, 8 May 1939.

Career as a player: Újpest Dozsa, Tatabányai Bányász.

Career as a coach: Újpest Dozsa (1985–88).

The extremely versatile Göröcs could play either in midfield or as an out-and-out striker. The programme for the Newcastle leg of the Cup Final was glowing in its praise of him: 'The oldest man in the team at 30. His great experience and exceptional ball-control have made him feared by defenders in all parts of the world. A wonderful midfield player, a tricky ball-juggler, he is included among the great Hungarian stars of all time. Has played for Hungary 58 times and took part in the 1966 World Cup in London.' It was glowing praise indeed and with a goal in the return leg in Budapest he lived up to this reputation.

János Göröcs.

English fans had probably first come across János in the 1962 World Cup Finals when he made one outing for Hungary (in a 6–1 win over Bulgaria), but he was more of a squad member than automatic selection at this stage. Experience and more regular selections came in due course and he ultimately played 62 matches for Hungary, and with 19 goals he can be well pleased with his contribution. Later in life he returned to Újpest as coach and steered the club to a Hungarian Cup Final success and to runners-up spot in the League.

Jim Scott's Recollections

Jim Scott.

'My great claim to fame is scoring Newcastle United's first-ever goal in Europe. We won that first leg against Dutch side Feyenoord 4–0, and that gave us the cushion we needed to travel to Holland. We lost 0–2 there so went through quite comfortably. People often underestimate this victory and forget that Feyenoord went on to win the European Cup the very next season. It was a smashing feeling to have beaten a side that even in 1968 we knew were very good. Mind you, they gave us a scare in Rotterdam and put us under a lot of pressure. Looking back it was as well we scored four at St James' Park as a four-goal deficit is almost impossible to pull back.

'Next up were Sporting Lisbon. We drew 1–1 over there and they only scored with five minutes to go. I had been over there with Hibernian in the Fairs Cup so I was familiar with the noise and atmosphere. You basically had to shut everything out of your mind and just go and play. I scored in that game too and then we won the return leg 1–0 at Newcastle, with Pop Robson scoring our goal. There were around 50,000 at St James' that night and that was the kind of enthusiasm there was for all of the subsequent games. Even getting within the vicinity of St James' Park on nights like those was near impossible for many folk. Fortunately, as a player you had a place reserved in the car park behind the main stand. What's more, I only stayed about a mile from the ground so getting to even the big games was no real hassle for me, but for some of the other lads it was a consideration and a worry in the lead up to games they could have done without.

'When we drew Zaragoza in the next round we knew we would be up against it. They had beaten many British teams in Europe and were recognised as being one of Spain's finest sides. We lost 3–2 over there; playing them quite bizarrely on New Year's Day! However, when we brought them back to Tyneside we beat them 2–1 in a dramatic night under the lights. It was snowing when we hammered Setúbal 5–1 and I think the weather really helped us. They were running around with gloves on and clearly not too impressed with the north-east weather.

'The semi-final paired us with Rangers. Given that I am a Scottish lad this was a tie that I really looked forward to. It was also a chance for my family to come and see me. The first game was at Ibrox and we drew 0–0 in a game that swung our way when Iam McFaul saved a penalty from Andy Penman. We felt confident that we would win the return game because we hardly ever lost at home. A good few of my family came down for the return leg and my brother Alex, who was living in Bury, came over as well.

'The night went well for me. I scored the first and Jackie Sinclair scored a real belter to put us 2–0 ahead. However, we were off the park for something like 20 minutes while the police tried to get the better of the Rangers fans. There was a very ugly atmosphere inside St James' that night and it was probably made worse by a tannoy announcement saying that further pitch invasions would see the tie abandoned. That was all the encouragement the Rangers fans needed!

'In the home leg of the Final we were actually drawing 0–0 at half-time and were struggling at that stage. Then our captain Bobby Moncur stepped forward and scored not just once, but twice. It was very unusual for him to score at all but he even scored in the return leg too. Those are the only three goals that I can remember him scoring!

'I didn't feel that we were quick out of the blocks in some of our games; although Pop Robson had some early goals. In the Final we were defending a decent lead to Újpest but we started the second leg very shakily – at one stage we looked as if we were going to lose. When we got into the dressing room at half-time Joe Harvey sat us down and was surprisingly calm. All he really said was that we should concentrate on going out and scoring the goal we needed to make them finally fold. "They will fold like a concertina" was the phrase he used. He was right, of course, and when we got that vital first goal we went on to win the game.

'We were presented with the Cup that night. We had a big support in Hungary with us and the atmosphere was marvellous – what a contrast to the all-British semi-final. Many of the players' families made it out and my wife was with Jackie Sinclair and Bobby Moncur's wives having travelled over on a supporters' plane. We went back to the hotel and drank all night. In fact, our wives missed the supporters' plane and came back on our plane.

'It was pandemonium when we got back to Newcastle. From Woolsington right into the city centre the streets were lined with cheering, happy people. It is fair to say we got invited to a good few places on the back of that win. In 1994 we actually got a civic reception – 25 years after winning the Cup.'

Interview with Bobby Moncur

Bobby, there were a few Scots in the Newcastle side that won the Fairs Cup, including yourself. How important was the Scottish contribution?
'You would have to say it was fairly vital. When big John McNamee played we had five Scots in the team. John was a new type of player for Newcastle, and it would be fair to say he was not a 'sophisticated' centre-half. He was very hard and I think he actually frightened a few of his opponents, and this was even more apparent in our English League fixtures. John was the sort of player who rolled his sleeves up and 'took no prisoners'; a tactic that proved remarkably effective!

'Jim Scott came to St James' as an old-fashioned outside-right. He was not a youngster but he was very skilful and he was great at taking players on and putting over telling crosses. He was remarkably like his brother Alex, who played for Rangers and Everton. Jackie Sinclair was a quietly effective player and, of course, grabbed a vital goal against Rangers in the semi-final at St James' Park. He wasn't as tricky as Jim Scott, nor was he as likely to go past full-backs, but his work-rate was excellent and he could track back when he didn't have the ball. Finally there was Tommy Gibb. What a worker Tommy was, he only seemed to know how to give 100 per cent and he was, along with Benny Arentoft, the engine room of that Newcastle United side.'

Bobby Moncur.

Speaking to your teammates from 1969 they, to a man, say you were a great captain. What do you think your strengths as a captain were?
'I was fortunate in that I was the second youngest player in the side [at 24] when we won that Final. I don't think I was the greatest player but I could make other players play to their maximum. The likes of Jim Scott and John McNamee were older than me but I wasn't bothered about giving them encouragement or instructions.'

How had you come to join Newcastle United?
'I was born in Perth and lived there until the age of nine, at which time my family moved to Kirkliston and I played Scottish football for West Lothian, and eventually I captained Scotland Schoolboys. I had a few options before joining Newcastle. I could have gone to either Hibs or Hearts and I had invites to go to Preston, Burnley and Wolverhampton. However, when I went to Newcastle United I instantly liked the feel of the place. The other factor was probably the city's close proximity to Scotland; I knew that while learning the game I would not be too far from home. I suppose the thing that swung it was the friendliness of the Geordies, even as a boy I realised that these were people I could live and work with.'

What part did the Newcastle support play in the Cup success?
'One of the major factors in our favour was the massive support we got at St James' Park. I don't remember too many defeats in all my years at Newcastle and we always felt as a group of players that the fans would back us. For those European games there was always around the 50,000 mark packed in and the atmosphere on European nights was really fantastic.'

Did you go into the Fairs Cup convinced you could win it?
'In truth we saw being in Europe as a huge bonus. Remember we had

qualified by finishing 10th in the League so there was no great build-up to qualifying. But I would say that the best Newcastle team I played in was the side that won the Fairs Cup. We had no prima donnas in that team and we played very much to our strengths.'

The Rangers game must have been a really dramatic occasion, what with it being an all-British semi-final.

'Yes, it was a huge draw at the time. Although, because I had never played in Scotland, it did not really affect me as much as the other lads. I remember listening to the draw for the semis and Jackie, Jim and John did not want to draw Rangers. When we walked into Ibrox Stadium for the first leg I could see that our Scots lads were nervous, I think they were so used to losing there with Scottish clubs. However, I knew in my heart that we had a really decent side and I was confident that we were playing in a much tougher League. I felt we could beat Rangers but I was concerned that some of our Scottish lads carried an inferiority complex into the game. As it turned out, of course, we drew 0–0 at Rangers with Iam McFaul saving a penalty. Ironically our Scots wingers Jim Scott and Jackie Sinclair then came up trumps at St James' in the second leg by scoring both goals. I remember after the game saying to them "Told you we would win!"'

In the Final Newcastle went to Hungary 3–0 up but were trailing 0–2 at half-time. Did you feel worried at that stage that it might slip away?

'Yes, we were all concerned when we went two goals down. We only conceeded 34 goals all season and we were good at the back, yet here we were seeing a great 3–0 lead disappearing before our eyes. They absolutely slaughtered us in the first half over there. At half-time Joe Harvey got us in the dressing room and simply said "all you have to do is score a goal and they will collapse." It was a short team talk and to the point...but he was spot on.'

You weren't known as a prolific marksman by any measure. Yet you scored three goals in the Final. Tell us a little about those goals?
'The first one at St James' Park came when I went upfield for a free-kick. I remember Wyn Davies had a shot blocked and ball fell to me and I blasted it in.

'The second one in that game came when I won the ball on the half-way line and played a one-two with someone. Then I played another one-two and suddenly I was right through. The ball bounced up nicely and someone shouted "hit it" so I did and in it flew!

'My third goal came in the second leg over in Hungary. It was just after half-time and we were desperate to pull a goal back. I went up for a corner-kick and it got knocked out, and Jackie Sinclair played it back in towards me and I simply volleyed it in.

'Amazingly I grabbed a fourth goal a couple of seasons later against Inter Milan in the same competition. So it is true that I scored more European goals for Newcastle than I did domestic goals.'

Appendices

Joe's Perfect Birthday Present

Joe Harvey.

How fitting it was that when Newcastle United won the Fairs Cup in June 1969 they did so on manager Joe Harvey's birthday. Given the huge role that the charismatic manager played in leading United to their finest triumph, the timing could hardly have been better.

Seven years earlier, in the summer of 1962, United had appointed Harvey as supremo in an act that brought a favourite son back to the club. Harvey's lustre as a former player was still strong in the 1960s and his appointment was widely acclaimed on Tyneside. The club were a Second Division outfit at the time but chairman Stan Seymour saw Harvey as just the man to lead the Magpies out of the doldrums. How Joe delivered.

Harvey had the perfect background for an aspiring Newcastle United boss. Although a Yorkshireman by birth (born Edlington, near Doncaster, on 6 November 1918), he became associated with United from 1945 onwards as a player. Signed for £4,250 from Bradford City in October 1945, he was an impressive man physically, standing at 6ft tall, and as a former army sergeant carried considerable military bearing. Within weeks of arriving at St James' he was made club captain and proved himself to be a fine leader of men. He went on to become the longest-serving club captain in Newcastle United's history.

His professional football career had begun in 1936 with Wolverhampton Wanderers but neither there nor at his next club, Bournemouth, was he able to make a real mark. He had better success at Bradford City, even scoring twice in one match against Newcastle, but his career was disrupted by the outbreak of World War Two. Although he did 'guest' for the likes of Aberdeen and Dundee United while on military service, in 1945 he returned to Bradford briefly before Newcastle snapped him up.

His arrival at the club heralded an upturn in fortunes. Promotion back to the top flight was followed by FA Cup Final victories in both 1951 and 1952. Capped three times by the Football League, he was an immensely popular captain and his habit of having a Guinness or two before a game and a half-time cigarette linked him to the terraces and marked him out as a man's man.

When his legendary power began to wane in 1953 he joined the backroom staff and he was very much part of the set-up at the club when the 1955 FA Cup was won. A deep thinker about the game, it was natural that he should wish to test himself as a manager and he did so at Barrow and Workington in Cumbria. By 1958 his stock was high enough to allow him to apply for the then vacant Newcastle job but he was pipped to the post by Charlie Mitten. It was another four years before he achieved his goal of managing his footballing love.

Gaining promotion was the bedrock upon which his 13-year tenure was built. He bought wisely and nurtured a productive youth system. The latter was vital, providing as it did talents such as Bobby Moncur and Pop Robson, key figures in the 1969 Fairs Cup triumph. David Craig was another of the home-reared Fairs Cup stars, and he was unstinting in his support of Harvey: 'I would have walked through a brick wall for Joe,' he once famously quipped.

Joe Harvey loved training sessions at Hunters Moor – where United prepared for their matches – and it was there that he prepared the set-pieces and tactics that marked Newcastle's style of the late 1960s.

Although unable to add to the Fairs Cup triumph, Harvey did bring Malcolm Macdonald to St James' Park in a move that did much to regenerate United's fortunes and standing. In paying £180,000 United were putting up the second biggest transfer fee in British football history, and the 21-year-old who became known as Super Mac really stirred the club into life.

Even when Harvey stepped down from the helm at the club in 1975 he remained at St James' Park, and when he died in February 1989 he was still part and parcel of the Newcastle United scene.

In 1964 Robert Hale Limited, a respected London publishing house, brought out a *Soccer Who's Who* compiled by Maurice Golesworthy. Here's what he had to say about Joe Harvey:

J. Harvey, Manager

Born Doncaster. Led Newcastle United into Division One in 1948 and to two FA Cup Final wins in 1951 and 1952, and returned to the club as manager in May 1962, hoping to lead them back into Division One again. A hard-working wing-half, he began his playing career with Wolverhampton Wanderers in 1936 but only had a season with them and one at Bournemouth before moving nearer home with Bradford City. Apart from good work in the half-back line he also made his mark in the attack at Valley Parade, and after the war Newcastle United got him for the bargain price of £4,250. That was in October 1945 and between then and the end of his playing career in 1953 he made over 200 appearances for United. He became the club's coach but left St James' Park in July 1955 to embark on a managerial career. His first post was with Barrow and after 20 months he moved to Workington, where he remained until being recruited to his favourite club on Tyneside in June 1962.

The Newcastle Squad

Professionals	*Date of Signing*	*Previous Club*	*Birthplace*
Allen, Geoffrey Barry	5 April 1963	Juniors	Newcastle
Arentoft, Preben	February 1969	Greenock Morton	Copenhagen
Augar, Tim	21 February 1968	Abingdon Utd	Oxford
Bennett, Albert	22 July 1965	Rotherham Utd	Durham
Burton, Alwyn Derek	7 June 1963	Norwich City	Chepstow
Clark, Frank Albert	30 October 1962	Crook Town	Highfield
Clarke, David Leslie	30 May 1967	Juniors	Newcastle
Cowan, John	13 February 1967	Crusaders	Belfast
Craggs, John Edward	8 April 1964	Juniors	Flint Hill
Craig, David James	5 August 1960	Juniors	Belfast
Davies, Ronald Wyn	27 October 1966	Bolton Wanderers	Caernarfon
Duffy, Alan	22 August 1966	Juniors	Stanley
Dyson, Keith	7 August 1968	Juniors	Blackhill
Elliott, David	29 December 1966	Sunderland	Tantobie
Ellison, Raymond	15 July 1966	Newcastle Schools	Newcastle
Foggon, Alan	31 July 1965	Juniors	West Pelton
Gibb, Thomas	5 August 1968	Partick Thistle	Bathgate
Guthrie, Ronald George	19 July 1963	Juniors	Burradon
Harrison, Tony	3 November 1967	Billingham	Thornaby
Hope, John	March 1969	Darlington	Shildon
Horsfield, Arthur	January 1969	Middlesbrough	Newcastle
Iley, James	6 September 1962	Nottingham Forest	South Kirkby
Johnson, Terrance	22 May 1967	Juniors	Newcastle
Lumsden, Arthur	28 September 1967	Longbenton	Newcastle
Marshall, Gordon	24 June 1963	Hearts	Farnham
Moncur, Robert	1 October 1960	Juniors	Perth
McFaul, William Stewart	10 November 1966	Linfield	Coleraine
McMahon, Kevin	11 August 1967	Consett	Tantobie
McNamee, John	30 December 1966	Hibernian	Coatbridge
Noble, Robert	30 July 1965	Juniors	Newcastle
Robson, Bryan Stanley	27 November 1962	Juniors	Sunderland
Robson, Thomas	30 December 1966	Chelsea	Gateshead
Ross, William Eric	2 August 1967	Glentoran	Belfast
Sinclair, Jackie	29 December 1967	Leicester City	Blairhall
Scott, James	1 August 1967	Hibernian	Falkirk
Winstanley, Graham	27 July 1964	Juniors	Croxdale
Young, David	10 September 1964	Juniors	Newcastle

The winning squad with the Fairs Cup.

The Newcastle Squad

Player Profiles

GEOFF ALLEN

Born: Newcastle, 10 November 1946.

Career as a player: NEWCASTLE UNITED.

A tricky winger, Geoff never quite managed to make the breakthrough at United, but his best season was certainly the Fairs Cup term. He played in two ties and against Feyenoord had one of those nights when he could do no wrong.

He was signed as a schoolboy in February 1964 and made his debut in a 2–0 home win over Norwich City. But that was his only game that term and in the very next season he again only made one appearance, again a 2–0 home win, this time against Cardiff City. In the 1966–67 season he made 10 League outings but was completely overlooked in the following campaign, but in 1968–69 he was in the thick of the early-season action. He played in both games against Feyenoord but by October 1968 he had picked up the injury that would end his career prematurely at the terribly young age of just 21.

PREBEN ARENTOFT

Born: Copenhagen, 1 November 1942.

Career as a player: Brønshøj, Greenock Morton, NEWCASTLE UNITED, Blackburn Rovers, Helsingborgs (Sweden).

An incredibly energetic midfielder, Preben 'Benny' Arentoft was the workhorse of the Newcastle United midfield. Born in 1942 in Copenhagen, Denmark, he played with Brønshøj and was a full Danish international with four caps (as well as two Under-19 caps and a single B award) by the time he joined Greenock Morton. At that time Morton were chaired by Hal Stewart, an innovative figure in the Scottish game who tapped into the previously under-exploited Scandinavian market. It was, however, a big decision for Danish players to move to Scotland (and several did) for they were no longer eligible to play for their country once they made this professional move.

In 1969 Arentoft swapped the west coast of Scotland for the east coast of England. He met United director Wilf Taylor, secretary Denis Baker and manager Joe Harvey in a hotel in Carlisle and it said that the Morton supremo Hal Stewart negotiated a £30,000 fee. Harvey was delighted with the purchase and conscious that he had pipped Tottenham, Chelsea and Southampton to securing the services of the industrious little Dane.

Arentoft's stay at St James' was not particularly long but he was a crucial member of the Fairs Cup team in the latter stages of the competition. Debut day saw Newcastle win 1–0 at Spurs and Preben had his first United goal a week later when he grabbed the opener in a 3–2 win over Sheffield Wednesday at St

James'. His major contribution to the Fairs Cup triumph was to grab the equaliser in Hungary when United fought back from 0–2 down to win famously 3–2. When Arentoft scored it was after a shot from Scott had been deflected into his path and he fairly buried the chance in the top right-hand corner.

He joined Blackburn Rovers for £25,000 in September 1971, the year in which he resurrected his international career and played against a Scotland side containing Newcastle captain Bobby Moncur. Benny finally gained nine Danish international caps, his last cap coming in June 1971 against West Germany when he was still a Newcastle player. Benny ended his senior career back in Scandinavia with Helsingborgs of Sweden, having made 63 Newcastle appearances and scored three goals. Although his midfield dynamism was his enduring legacy, some fans prefer to recall the day he replaced an injured Iam McFaul in goal during a 5–1 win over Manchester United in 1970.

It is interesting to note that when Preben's Denmark career ended in 1971 players were extremely well travelled. The 11 Danish players that started the game against West Germany were earning their living as follows: one in Scotland, three in Germany, one in Holland, one in France, one in Belgium, three in Denmark and, of course, Benny himself in England.

Preben Arentoft was the head of child probation for the city council of Copenhagen and a prominent art dealer, but he has since retired.

Season	**Appearances**	**Goals**
1968–69	14	3
1969–70	27 (5)	0
1970–71	18	0
Total	**59 (5)**	**3**

ALBERT BENNETT

Born: Chester-le-Street, 16 July 1944.

Career as a player: Rotherham United, NEWCASTLE UNITED, Norwich City.

A slim inside-forward, debut day for Albert came in August 1965 when he turned out in a 0–1 defeat to Sheffield Wednesday. As if that was not bad enough, in his next appearance the Magpies were thrashed 0–4 by Stoke City. But Albert was made of stern stuff and a few weeks later he embarked up on a run that saw him score in three consecutive games.

For all he was a fairly useful marksman he never seemed to quite fit, and although he scored in a derby win over Sunderland Newcastle's number eight was on his way out of St James' in early 1969. That said, he had undergone a cartilage operation and when he tried to come back at the start of the 1968–69 campaign he broke down; in some quarters this was reckoned to be the driver behind Tommy Gibb being signed from Partick Thistle. His contribution to the Inter-Cities Fairs Cup run was to play against Sporting Lisbon as a sub in the 1–0 home win.

Bought for £27,000, he was sold for only £2,000 less when he joined Norwich City in 1969.

Season	**Appearances**	**Goals**
1965–66	26	10
1966–67	32	3
1967–68	28	10
1968–69	3 (1)	0
Total	**89 (1)**	**23**

ALWYN 'OLLIE' BURTON

Born: Chepstow, 11 November 1941.

Career as a player: Newport County, Norwich City, NEWCASTLE UNITED.

Ollie Burton's first senior club was Newport County, whom he joined in 1958. After three outstanding years he was sold to Norwich City for £12,000 in May 1961 while still a teenager. He won a League Cup-winners' medal in Norfolk, and scored at Sunderland en route to the Final, but perhaps more significant was a scintillating display against Newcastle in the FA Cup fourth round when Norwich romped home 5–0.

Predictably, Welsh Under-23 caps followed for this talented sportsman (he was also a useful tennis player), and when he added two full caps it was clear he had the talent to go to the very top. Newcastle United paid a fee in the region of £25,000 in June 1963 to take the big-hearted Welshman to Tyneside. He had made 73 senior appearances for the Canaries and netted nine goals.

Ollie ultimately took his full caps tally to nine and was rewarded for his outstanding contribution to Newcastle with a testimonial match against Sunderland just after the Wearsiders had won the 1973 FA Cup.

Burton played a vital role in the Fairs Cup triumph and was extremely reliable and versatile when called upon. Of course, this should have been no surprise for he had played as both a centre-forward and a right-back earlier in his career and had been capped at Under-23 level by Wales in both positions.

A knee injury ended Ollie's playing career in 1972 and thereafter he earned his living as a brewery representative before opening his own fast-food outlet when he returned to Norwich. Ollie was actually christened Alwyn, but in keeping with football tradition the world over was given a rather less 'demanding' name!

Season	**Appearances**	**Goals**
1963–64	19	3
1964–65	2	1
1965–66	18 (1)	0
1966–67	17 (1)	0
1967–68	37 (3)	3
1968–69	49 (1)	1
1969–70	35 (2)	0
1970–71	17 (1)	0
1971–72	22	0
Total	**216 (9)**	**8**

FRANK CLARK

Born: Rowlands Gill, 9 September 1943.

Career as a player: Crook Town, NEWCASTLE UNITED, Nottingham Forest.

Career as a manager: Orient, Nottingham Forest, Manchester City.

Born near Gateshead, Frank Albert Clark was highly sought-after as a young player. His performances with local non-League club Crook Town were very promising and he represented them in the FA Amateur Cup

Final at Wembley. He rejected overtures from Sunderland and Preston North End and plumped to join Newcastle. An early setback came in the form of a leg-break but by 1965 he was celebrating a Second Division Championship medal. He went from strength to strength and made over 450 outings as a Magpie.

In the 1968–69 season Frank was handed the club captaincy while Bobby Moncur was recuperating from an operation. Granted a free transfer in 1975, he enjoyed unprecedented success with his next club, Nottingham Forest. Incredibly, he added English Championship, League Cup and, most impressively of all, European Cup medals to his collection of honours.

He returned to the North East in 1979 with Sunderland – as assistant manager to Ken Knighton. He held the same posts at Nottingham Forest and Orient before becoming Orient manager in his own right in May 1983. Although he struggled to find success, he became managing director of the London club in 1986. Seven years later he replaced the inimitable Brian Clough as Forest manager and by 1996 he was boss of Manchester City; by this stage his stock as a quality manager was rising considerably. Moreover, Frank was also a major figure in the League Managers' Association.

Looking back on Frank's career it is difficult not to comment on his lack of goals and the fact that two he did score came within weeks of each other! In October 1973 he was on the score sheet against Doncaster

Rovers in a League Cup tie and clearly enthused by the experience he repeated it in a Texaco Cup tie against Birmingham City in December.

Bobby Moncur said of Frank that 'He was probably unlucky not to get a full England cap. He was a strong player and a thoughtful one, and he carried that thoughtful approach into his managerial career at Nottingham Forest and Manchester City.'

Season	**Appearances**	**Goals**
1963–64	2	0
1964–65	44	0
1965–66	38 (1)	0
1966–67	42	0
1967–68	37	0
1968–69	54	1
1969–70	40	0
1970–71	37	0
1971–72	45	1
1972–73	54	0
1973–74	56	2
1974–75	29 (1)	0
Total	**478 (2)**	**4**

DAVE CLARKE

Born: Newcastle, 24 July 1949.

Career as a player: NEWCASTLE UNITED, Doncaster Rovers, Darlington, South Shields, Blyth Spartans.

Take a look at the team picture that appeared in the *Newcastle Chronicle* of 19 November 1968 and in the back row are two goalkeepers either side of coach Dave Smith. The names read Iam McFaul and Dave Clarke. McFaul, of course, went on to play in each and every fixture en route to the marvellous win over Újpest, but Clarke, on the other hand, is a player with considerably less United heritage. He was named as substitute goalkeeper, for example, in the home tie with Sporting Lisbon but did not play that night or indeed in a single League fixture, and it would be fair to say his was a career that never really took off at St James' Park.

Bizarrely there is, nevertheless, little doubt that Dave's football highlight did occur at St James' Park...but it came in 1978 when he was in the Blyth Spartans side that, as a non-League team, battled Wrexham in a famous fifth-round FA Cup tie watched by around 42,000 with several thousand locked out. Perhaps even more remarkably it would have been Newcastle against Blyth Spartans had United not fallen heavily to the Welsh side in round four. Dave won 16 non-League England international caps and the Northern League was perhaps his most appropriate stage.

That said, he did try very hard to break into League football. He spent part of the 1969–70 season on loan to Darlington where he played in 11 matches, and he also had three outings for Doncaster Rovers. Finally he found his niche in non-League football in the North East, initially as a player and then as a coach.

JOHN CRAGGS

Born: Flint Hill, 31 October 1948.

Career as a player: NEWCASTLE UNITED, Middlesbrough, NEWCASTLE UNITED, Darlington.

With over 400 outings for Middlesbrough to his name there is no doubt that John is best known as a Boro legend. Yet it all started so promisingly at St James' Park for this England Youth cap. An effective, popular full-

back, he had 50 United appearances under his belt when surprisingly he was sold for £60,000 to Middlesbrough in 1971, and had he not been vying with David Craig for the number-two jersey he would certainly have made many more Magpie starts. He won promotion on Teesside in 1974 and was a vital cog in Jack Charlton's very effective First Division team. He was there for an entire decade before he made a surprise return to Tyneside for a season.

John flitted in and out of United's Fairs Cup run, and in the run-up to the Rangers match there were doubts expressed about Craggs' abilities. In-between the two Rangers clashes he had played in the final League game of the season against Liverpool and been given a torrid time by England winger Peter Thompson. But in the big European nights he was very effective and gave some of his finest displays in a Newcastle strip.

John was given a testimonial by Boro and ended his career after his second stint at Newcastle with a decent spell at Darlington. When his playing career was over he retired in Middlesbrough.

DAVID CRAIG

Born: Belfast, 8 June 1944.

Career as a player: NEWCASTLE UNITED.

A one-club man, Belfast-born David was the right-back in Newcastle's Fairs Cup team. He joined United as a teenager in early 1960s straight from school as an apprentice and enjoyed a lengthy career at St James'

Park, playing 351 League games as a Magpie and well over 400 competitive games. His qualities were such that he won 25 Northern Ireland international caps.

David made his debut in November 1963 when United were a Second Division club, although it was on League Cup duty against Bournemouth that he first stepped into the first team. Those were difficult days for United as evidenced by early 4–0 thumpings from Cardiff and Bury, hardly the stuff to convince young David that he was at the right club. It is interesting to note that David was at the club before Joe Harvey arrived in his managerial capacity and could certainly reflect on both the good and the bad times. Ultimately, very few players in the history of Newcastle United made more Magpie outings than the ever reliable David.

He played a key role in United landing the Fairs Cup but injured his knee in the game against Zaragoza and was only able to return to first-team duty for the latter stages of the tournament. When time was up on his spell on Tyneside (his last game was against Arsenal in November 1977) be briefly joined Blyth Spartans, and he later worked as both a milkman and a newsagent in North Shields.

David had an interesting international career, making his bow in 1967 against Wales and enjoying a sustained run in the side in the late 1960s, then reverting from right-back to left-back as the Irish solved their dilemma of how to field Craig and Pat Rice in the same side.

Such was the high regard that David was held in by United he was awarded a testimonial match, and on 30 April 1975 he led Newcastle out against Sunderland in a benefit fixture.

Season	**Appearances**	**Goals**
1963–64	14	0
1964–65	42	0
1965–66	40	1
1966–67	26	1
1967–68	10 (1)	0
1968–69	38	1
1969–70	33	1
1970–71	38	1
1971–72	41	1
1972–73	54	5
1973–74	38 (1)	1
1974–75	16 (2)	0
1975–76	20	1
1976–77	3 (2)	0
1977–78	8	0
Total	**421 (6)**	**13**

WYN DAVIES

Born: Caernarfon, 20 March 1942.

Career as a player: Deiniolen, Llanberis, CaernarfonTown, Wrexham, Bolton Wanderers, NEWCASTLE UNITED, Manchester City, Manchester United, Blackpool, Crystal Palace (on loan), Stockport County, Crewe Alexandra, Bangor City.

Wyn started his professional career with Wrexham, where he won the Welsh Youth Cup in 1960 and scored three in a famous 10–1 win over the North East's Hartlepool. Such exploits earned him a move to Bolton in 1962 for £25,000. A tall target-man with an uncanny ability in the air, in 155 League games for the Trotters he scored 66 goals.

It cost Newcastle United £80,000 to add the 26-year-old striker to their attack and he had a spine-tingling derby debut against Sunderland. He was known as 'Wyn the Leap' due to his marvellous aerial ability and his antics spawned a series of terrace anthems. The most famous of these was based on the Manfred Mann and Bob Dylan hit *The Mighty Quinn*, with United's choir singing 'Come on without, Come on within, you've not seen nothing like the mighty Wyn'. There are some who suggested Davies' footballing style was more akin to the 1950s and early 1960s. What is for certain is that his aggressive and physical style of play unsettled some Continental defenders. It is a sign of the times that when he first joined Newcastle he stayed in a boarding house in Heaton!

His role in landing the Fairs Cup is hard to over-exaggerate, and equally he did much to help Bryan 'Pop' Robson establish himself. Some said that Davies was Joe Harvey's best signing. Davies played in 24 European ties for United and scored 10 times. He was revered on Tyneside and when he left to join Manchester City in 1971 he did so with 40 goals in 180 league games to his name. He played more matches for Newcastle than any of his other senior clubs. Amazingly, in September 1972 he switched to Manchester United but by that stage his career was on a gradual decline and he served a number of small clubs before moving to non-League football with Bangor City. Wyn played for Wales in 34 international fixtures from 1964 and scored six goals.

After football he worked for the bakery firm Warburtons back in Bolton. Captain Bobby Moncur rated Davies in the near-unique class: 'Wyn was quite simply a phenomenal jumper and header. I have never seen anyone since that could jump so high and hang there like he did. He scored a lot of goals for us in Europe and the Continentals were nonplussed by his style.'

Season	Appearances	Goals
1966–67	30	9
1967–68	43	12
1968–69	52	15
1969–70	50	11
1970–71	41	6
Total	**216**	**53**

KEITH DYSON

Born: Consett, 10 February 1950.

Career as a player: NEWCASTLE UNITED, Carlisle United, Brighton, Carlisle United.

Keith made his United debut in September 1968 against Tottenham Hotspur and a few weeks later enjoyed a run of three games in which he scored each time. He played in both games against Real Zaragoza and made 10

European outings in total. His early progress won him England Under-23 caps but somehow his Newcastle career petered out.

He was transferred to Blackpool in October 1971 as a makeweight in the deal that brought the exciting Tony Green to Newcastle. He recovered much of his skill at Blackpool and in 94 games for the Tangerines he scored 30 times. However, a knee injury all but ended his football ambitions and he moved the short distance to Lancaster in 1976 to play non-League football before sampling football in America with Cleveland Cobras.

Season	**Appearances**	**Goals**
1968–69	21 (1)	6
1969–70	26 (1)	13
1970–71	39 (1)	7
1971–72	6 (1)	1
Total	**92 (4)**	**27**

DAVID ELLIOTT

Born: Tantobie, 10 February 1945.

Career as a player: Gateshead, Sunderland, NEWCASTLE UNITED, Southend, Newport County, Bangor City, Newport County.

Signed in December 1966 from Sunderland, David made his debut in the same match as big John McNamee on the last day of 1966 away to Spurs. David cost United just £10,000 and that proved good value, particularly in the 1967–68 season when he played in over 40 matches.

His Sunderland debut came in 1964 against Derby County and he played 35 matches for the Rokerites before being lured to Newcastle. He played far fewer games in the Inter-Cities season but did start in three of

the European ties, and against Sporting Lisbon he gave one of his finest displays in a Newcastle shirt.

He played his last game for United at home to Ipswich Town in November 1970 and moved to Southend in February 1971 on a free transfer. This was to be his most productive club; between 1970 and 1974 he turned out in almost 200 games for the Essex outfit.

Season	Appearances	Goals
1966–67	18	0
1967–68	42	3
1968–69	19 (2)	0
1969–70	6 (2)	1
1970–71	1	0
Total	**86 (4)**	**4**

ALAN FOGGON

Born: Chester-le-Street, 23 February 1950.

Career as a player: NEWCASTLE UNITED, Cardiff City, Middlesbrough, Manchester United, Sunderland, Southend United, Hartlepool United (on loan).

Alan Foggon was only 19 when he scored in the Fairs Cup Final. His is a story that seems stranger than fiction. He also earned a degree of fame as a player who served all three big north-east clubs – Newcastle, Middlesbrough

and Sunderland. In terms of his Newcastle career his goal in the second leg of the Fairs Cup Final was his high point, but ultimately his career at United flattered to decieve.

Alan was only 15 when he joined Newcastle but that Cup Final goal apart he failed to build upon the undoubted promise he displayed. He made his debut against Arsenal in Feburary 1968, scored his first goal for the club against Nottingham Forest days later and ended the season brandishing a Fairs Cup-winners' badge. Nothing, it seemed, could stop the young lad with flowing black locks and pop star looks.

Yet by April 1971 he was on his way from Tyneside. His last appearance came on 24 April in a 1–1 draw with West Ham United and over the summer a deal was negotiated which took him to Cardiff City for £25,000. The simple problem he had at Newcastle was a lack of consistency.

Alan never really settled in Wales but he had far more success when he returned north to join Middlesbrough. His 128 games for Boro yielded 50 goals and he linked well in a solid team that boasted talents like John Hickton and Bobby Murdoch.

From Boro it was on to Manchester United and then he joined Sunderland in September 1976 but failed to impress in Bob Stokoe's team, and in truth the departure of Stokoe from the managerial office did not help his cause. The new Sunderland manager Ian MacFarlane (who would be succeeded by Jimmy Adamson) seemingly did not take to Foggon's style.

It transpired that Alan was not really cut out for professional football and by the age of 28 he had left the game completely. Rarely has a player promised so much and sadly fizzled out. Still, with a goal in a winning Cup Final and a peg at Old Trafford to look back on, his is a tale not without highlights.

Season	Appearances	Goals
1967–68	1	0
1968–69	28 (7)	7
1969–70	27 (2)	5
1970–71	14 (7)	4
Total	**70 (16)**	**16**

TOMMY GIBB

Born: Bathgate, 13 December 1944.
Career as a player: Wallhouse Rose, Armadale Thistle, Partick Thistle, NEWCASTLE UNITED, Sunderland, Hartlepool.

Tommy was the last major signing Joe Harvey made in the run-up to the Fairs Cup season (Benny Arentoft arrived during the campaign). Signed as a right-half from Partick Thistle for £25,000 in August 1968, he had been one of the Scottish game's most sought-after talents. His apprenticeship in Scotland had been spent at Junior League side Armadale, which had also given a start to the likes of Joe Baker, Colin Stein and George Farm. When Gibb was 18 he graduated to Glasgow club Partick Thistle and made steady progress there, and such was his progress that Newcastle were caught in something of an auction for his transfer when they tried to sign him.

Tommy made his Newcastle debut early in the 1968–69 season against Sheffield Wednesday at Hillsborough, and in his home debut a week later against Chelsea he stunned all and sundry with a wonderful long-distance goal. Thereafter his lanky frame was a permanent fixture in the side for 170

games. He contributed substantially to the Fairs Cup triumph by scoring three times in the successful run and, indeed, managed to play in 24 consecutive European ties for United.

Joe Harvey was always a big Gibb fan. On the eve of the ties with Rangers in the Fairs Cup semi-final he was displeased with suggestions in some quarters of the Scottish sporting press that Gibb was an ordinary player. Harvey retorted: 'You will see a completely new Tommy Gibb, he has made tremendous strides since he moved to Tyneside.' For Rangers assistant manager Willie Thornton this was no real surprise. Thornton had been the Partick Thistle manager when Gibb was sold to Newcastle and negotiated a down payment of £25,000 with a further £10,000 factored in as a fee due when Gibb had played 10 first-team games. Thornton was shrewd, and when asked why he had negotiated this then unusual clause, he responded: 'I won't have long to wait for the next cheque,' and he was right!

But by 1970 the crowd at St James' were on Gibb's back and for a spell he was reduced to playing in away matches only. One press report of the day noted that 'the lunatic fringe at Gallowgate have got it in for him'. In June 1975 he was granted a free transfer and moved the short distance down the A19 to Sunderland, but he played in only 10 games for the Black Cats in the 1975–76 season before he moved to Hartlepool in July 1977.

After football he trained to be a lorry driver and was working in that capacity when a back injury forced him to retire. By that time he was living in West Lothian. When I quizzed Bobby Moncur about Tommy Gibb the captain was unstinting in his praise: 'Tommy was the unsung hero of the side in that he was prepared to work very hard and take a lot of aggravation on behalf of the team. He would be up and down the park for the entire 90 minutes, working non-stop.'

Season	**Appearances**	**Goals**
1968–69	58	6
1969–70	52	1
1970–71	49	2
1971–72	27 (3)	1
1972–73	20	4
1973–74	24 (9)	4
1974–75	17(3)	0
Total	**247 (15)**	**18**

RON GUTHRIE

Born: Newcastle, 19 April 1944.
Career as a player: NEWCASTLE UNITED, Sunderland, Blyth Spartans, Ashington.

An FA Cup-winner with Sunderland in 1973, Ron had actually enjoyed a decade with Newcastle before moving to Roker Park. With David Craig and Frank Clark establishing such solid Newcastle careers, Ron's task was always going to be a huge one, and in January 1973 he accepted an offer from Bob Stokoe to move down the road to Sunderland. His timing was immaculate; he scored in the FA Cup quarter-final against Luton Town and then picked up a winners' badge against Don Revie's all-conquering Leeds in May 1973.

Ron played in several European games for United, but three of them – against Southampton, Anderlecht and Porto – came in the 1969–70 season. His solitary contribution to the Inter-Cities triumph came when he emerged as a substitute against Real Zaragoza in the tight 2–1 win. But although he replaced David Craig that night, and started the next match against Arsenal, he was not able to command the jersey for the remainder of the season and ultimately lost out to David Elliott.

Guthrie wound down his career by going to South Africa and then returning to his homeland to star with Blyth Spartans and Ashington in non-League football.

Season	**Appearances**	**Goals**
1966–67	5 (1)	0
1967–68	4 (1)	0
1968–69	6 (1)	0
1969–70	17 (2)	1
1970–71	13 (2)	0
1971–72	9	0
1972–73	4	1
Total	**58 (7)**	**2**

JOHN HOPE

Born: Shildon, 30 March 1949.

Career as a player: Darlington, NEWCASTLE UNITED, Sheffield United, Hartlepool United, Whitby Town.

As Newcastle set about sweeping Vitória Setúbal out of the Fairs Cup they were working in the background to line up teenage Darlington goalkeeper John Hope. Indeed, so keen were the club to secure the signature of young

Hope that United director Stan Seymour and chief scout Temple Lisle missed the 5–1 thrashing of Setúbal to watch the 'keeper perform in a reserve fixture for Darlington against Hartlepool.

The records show that Hope was signed by Joe Harvey in March 1969 for a fee in the region of £8,000 (quite an outlay on a youngster who had but 14 appearances for Darlington under his belt by this stage) but for all the determination in luring him to Tyneside John would make only one League appearance for United.

Predictably he enjoyed greater success at his next club – Second Division Sheffield United – whom he joined halfway through the 1970–71 campaign. This was impeccable timing as United were destined to finish second and gain promotion to the top flight. He replaced veteran Alan Hodgkinson in goal (at a time when Hodgkinson had over 550 Sheffield United appearances to his name) and in keeping seven consecutive clean sheets in the promotion run-in cemented his place at the club. Back in the First Division, Hope played in two victories over Newcastle in the 1971–72 campaign, and Sheffield finished above the Magpies in the League so John could be well pleased with his switch.

Interestingly, John Hope's move to the Blades (along with David Ford) eased the passage of Sheffield striker John Tudor to St James' Park. In the summer of 1975 Hope joined his final club in the senior game when he switched to Hartlepool.

ARTHUR HORSFIELD

Born: Newcastle, 5 July 1946.

Career as a player: Middlesbrough, NEWCASTLE UNITED, Swindon Town, Charlton Athletic, Watford.

There is a suspicion that had Arthur Horsfield been a little less feisty he might have made more of his footballing career. As it was he succeeded at

most of his clubs but he left more than one under a cloud; although if you had taken away that combative nature then chances are he wouldn't have been half as prolific.

A former Middlesbrough apprentice, Arthur made a name for himself at Ayresome Park where he scored 51 League goals in little over 100 games. His debut was the stuff of Teesside folklore as he scored after just three minutes, only for the game to be abandoned and struck from the records. In January 1969 he moved to Newcastle having fallen from favour with the then Boro manager, and former Newcastle star, Stan Anderson. It cost United boss Joe Harvey in the region of £17,500 to bring Arthur north.

His stay on Tyneside was a short one which lasted only for the 1968–69 season. He played one game in the successful Inter-Cities Fairs Cup run, at inside-right in the sensational 5–1 win over Portugal's Vitória Setúbal. Goals against Spurs, Burnley and Sheffield Wednesday were his contribution to the League campaign, but, frustrated by a lack of first-team openings (Wyn Davies was the preferred striker), he moved on in the summer of 1969.

Horsfield showed a degree of ambition and bravery when he left to join shock League Cup winners Swindon Town in 1969. The little Wiltshire club were a Third Division club at the time and Arthur added a degree of drive to their forward line; indeed, he topped their scoring charts in his first season there and won the Anglo-Italian Cup with them. In 1972 he moved to London to join Charlton Athletic. In 1975 he joined Watford but ended his career with Dartford in non-League football.

Season	Appearances	Goals
1968–69	8 (2)	3
Total	**8 (2)**	**3**

JIM ILEY

Born: South Kirkby, 15 December 1935.

Career as a player: Tottenham Hotspur, Nottingham Forest, NEWCASTLE UNITED, Peterborough United.

Career as a manager: Peterborough United, Barnsley, Blackburn Rovers, Bury, Exeter City.

Vastly experienced, Jim left the club just weeks after Newcastle had ousted Feyenoord from the Inter-Cities Fairs Cup. His only outing in the tournament had come as a substitute in the ferocious onslaught United suffered away in Rotterdam.

His senior playing career had begun in London with Spurs but in July 1959 he joined Nottingham Forest for £16,000 and thus missed out on being part of the White Hart Lane side that memorably won the double in 1961. Nevertheless, he settled well at Forest and made 103 appearances until he switched to Newcastle in 1962.

A cultured, ball playing left-half, he helped United back into the top flight in 1965 after polishing his skills in the harsh world of Second Division football. In the promotion season he chipped in with a few goals and at one stage captained the club. He joined Peterborough in January 1969 to take up a role as player-manager. This lasted for three years and he impressed sufficiently to earn a post as boss of Barnsley in 1973. He left Oakwell to join Blackburn Rovers in April 1978. Between July 1980 and February 1984 he was boss of Bury and he followed this with a spell in charge of Exeter City.

Season	**Appearances**	**Goals**
1962–63	38	0
1963–64	45	3
1964–65	40	5
1965–66	42	4
1966–67	37	0
1967–68	38 (1)	4
1968–69	2 (5)	0
Total	**242 (6)**	**16**

WILLIAM 'IAM' McFAUL

Born: Coleraine, 10 January 1943.

Career as a player: Coleraine, Linfield, NEWCASTLE UNITED.

Career as a manager: NEWCASTLE UNITED, Guam.

A most agile custodian, McFaul was born in Coleraine in 1943 and joined Newcastle in 1966. This was a rather surprising move when the detail is examined. For while McFaul had indeed played against Newcastle United, and therefore had a chance to impress manager Joe Harvey, it is rather surprising to learn that the game in question saw Newcastle beat Linfield 7–2! Still, for £7,000 Harvey made McFaul a Newcastle United player.

McFaul's had been classic progress, building up from Irish Youth caps though to Amateur caps and eventually full international awards. He had won a Championship medal with Belfast-based Linfield in 1966 and was clearly destined for bigger and better things. He settled well on Tyneside and ultimately joined that band of men who have both played for and managed the club. Such longevity was hard to imagine in November 1966 as McFaul made his debut against Liverpool and struggled to shake off Gordon Marshall's ambitions for the number-one jersey at St James' Park.

His time with Newcastle was strange in that he made what can best be called a 'faltering' start. Yet by the time he ended his playing career he had won a Fairs Cup badge, two Texaco Cup medals, an Anglo-Italian Cup medal and played in an FA Cup Final. Five of his six Northern Ireland caps came after Newcastle had won the Fairs Cup.

Iam played a full role in the Fairs Cup triumph. Not only did play in every single match but he also rose in stature as the competition progressed. In the semi-final he famously saved an Andy Penman penalty (after conceding the award himself), and in the Final against Újpest he was often a one-man barrier against the lively Hungarians.

In April 1974 he added a Texaco Cup-winners' badge to his medal collection when he played in the side that beat Burnley 2–1 at St James' Park (Clark, Moncur and Gibb were fellow survivors from the Fairs Cup Final). He played in a few bizarre matches too, including a 5–4 defeat at Ipswich's Portman Road not long before he hung up his boots.

After playing in 290 League games for the Magpies he joined Newcastle's coaching staff and he was ultimately United manager from 1985 to 1988. Later he served Coleraine in the same capacity and he was Northern Ireland's goalkeeping coach for three years in the mid-1990s. In 2000 he took on the challenge of managing Guam in the Pacific Islands and he spent three years there (a difficult job as 19–0 defeats to both China and Iran proved) until returning to Ireland to work with Omagh Town and then the Irish FA.

Season	**Appearances**	**Goals**
1966–67	8	–
1967–68	5	–
1968–69	58	–
1969–70	52	–
1970–71	48	–
1971–72	46	–
1972–73	45	–
1973–74	61	–
1974–75	55	–
1975–76	2	–
Total	**380**	**0**

JOHN McNAMEE

Born: Coatbridge, 11 June 1941.

Career as a player: Bellshill Juniors, Celtic, Hibernian, NEWCASTLE UNITED, Blackburn Rovers, Hartlepool United, Morton, Lancaster City, Workington Town.

Career as a manager: Workington Town.

A powerful, hulking centre-half, McNamee was a frightening figure when in his full glory and many a centre-forward was apprehensive about facing this 'robust' defender. Born in Coatbridge, Lanarkshire – a hot-bed of Celtic support – he moved from Bellshill Juniors to Celtic in 1959. By 1963 he was playing at centre-half in a Scottish Cup Final and vying with the legendary Billy McNeill to play pivot in the Parkhead team.

In April 1964 he moved to Hibernian but was only there for a couple of years before Joe Harvey took him to Tyneside in a £26,000 deal. Harvey is attributed with a famous quote that suggested 'the first time I met John McNamee I ducked' – such was the aggressive demeanor of the big Scotsman. This sounds just about right. At Celtic McNamee was so enraged by a colleague repeatedly driving past him at a bus-stop (when players did not all have cars) that he turned training into a mini war zone (incidentally, that player was John Hughes, who would later play down the road at Sunderland – as did his brother Billy).

McNamee made his United debut on the last day of 1966 in an away League fixture at Tottenham. His stint at Gallowgate was his longest in senior football, spending five years as an honorary Geordie and playing in 115 League games. One of his finest matches must be the first leg semi-final in Glasgow against Rangers. Up against Scotland's first £100,000 footballer, Colin Stein, he was imperious and cleverly shackled the Scottish striker. Alas, he aggravated a thigh strain in that game which not only kept him out of the second leg but also meant that he lost his place for the Final too.

Sold to Blackburn in November 1971 for £15,000, he later played with Morton and then Lancaster City before briefly managing Workington Town.

Season	Appearances	Goals
1966–67	21	1
1967–68	33	2
1968–69	27 (2)	3
1969–70	17 (1)	1
1970–71	30	1
1971–72	2	0
Total	**130 (3)**	**8**

GORDON MARSHALL

Born: Farnham (Surrey), 2 July 1939.

Career as a player: Balgreen Rovers, Dalkeith Thistle, Heart of Midlothian, NEWCASTLE UNITED, Nottingham Forest, Hibernian, Celtic, Aberdeen, Arbroath.

While playing with Edinburgh-based Hearts, 6ft 1in Gordon Marshall won two League Championship medals, a League Cup-winners' badge and an England Under-23 cap. He had joined Hearts in August 1956 and in November of that year made his competitive first-team bow against Kilmarnock (but he did play in a friendly against – of all teams – Newcastle United at St James' Park on 19 September 1956). He was quickly recognised as one of the most highly-rated custodians north of border and when Newcastle swooped in June 1963 they had to write a cheque for

£18,000. Between 1963 and October 1968 Gordon was a regular at Newcastle and he made 177 appearances on League duty alone for the Magpies. He left the club for £17,500, just as the Fairs Cup run was gathering momentum, in order to join Nottingham Forest, and thus it was Iam McFaul who earned the plaudits as United's goalkeeper in the triumphant run.

In 1969 Gordon returned to Scotland and Edinburgh, but this time to join Hibernian. Signed by Bob Shankly, the brother of the legendary Liverpool boss, he made a dreadful start in which he conceeded two goals within six minutes of his debut.

After leaving Hibs he joined Celtic, Aberdeen and then Arbroath and took his total Scottish League appearances to just under the 400 mark. Gordon retired in 1978 and concentrated on business interests in newsagents and hairdressers, but his son (also called Gordon) became a noted goalkeeper too, playing with the likes of Kilmarnock and Celtic...and also spending a spell with Rangers!

BOBBY MONCUR

Born: Perth, 19 January 1945.
Career as a player: NEWCASTLE UNITED, Sunderland, Carlisle United.
Career as a manager: Carlisle United, Heart of Midlothian, Plymouth Argyle.

Born in the sleepy Scottish market town of Perth, Bobby was a wonderfully skilled defender who earned a special place in the history of Newcastle United when he discovered a scoring touch in the Inter-Cities Fairs Cup Final. Above and beyond that he played over 300 games as a Magpie and captained both Newcastle and Scotland. He was, in fact, a very talented all-round sportsman and like 'Pop' Robson was a winner of the

Professional Footballers' Golf Championship (no mean feat given the size and quality of the competition).

Signed as an apprentice when only 15, he came to the club with quite a reputation having won five caps for Scotland's Schoolboy international side. He lived up to expectations, however, as in 1962 he captained United to the FA Youth Cup and scored in the Final. Bobby made his senior United debut at the tail end of the 1962–63 campaign and over the next few seasons he gathered experience in the Second Division. When Newcastle stormed back into the top flight Bobby had learnt his craft and for nine seasons he was a major part of the first-team scene. His final game for Newcastle was in the 1974 FA Cup Final against Liverpool which the club lost 0–3.

The momentous 1968–69 season actually started badly for Bobby as he battled to overcome a cartilage operation, yet he did so with customary determination. It was astonishing that he should fail to score for the club until the 1969 Fairs Cup Final against Újpest, and to score in both games made his entry to the scoring game all the more sensational. With his elegant build – he was rather like the Chappell brothers of Australian cricketing fame – he was robust but rarely in trouble with referees. He was capped by Scotland while at Newcastle (against Holland in May 1968) and went on to pick up 16 caps. Two of those caps were against England and a couple against Wales, but interestingly he did not come up against teammate Wyn Davies in the matches against the Welsh.

Always a compassionate man, Bobby played for a Scotland XI in the match against a Rangers-Celtic select to aid victims and their relatives following the dreadful Ibrox disaster in which 66 fans were killed. In the summer of 1974 he made the short move east to Sunderland where another ex-Newcastle hero – Bob Stokoe – was manager. He was an ever present in his first season on Wearside and is credited with helping Dave Watson become one of the most accomplished central-defenders in England. By this stage 'Pop' Robson was also a Sunderland regular, and inspired perhaps by Robson's prolific strike-rate Bobby popped in a couple of goals as a Sunderland player. He was the Rokerites' Player of the Year in 1976 but in November of that year Bobby moved to Carlisle, initially as player-manager and then from September 1977 he was concentrating solely on management.

His appointment as Hearts boss in February 1980 brought him into contact with John Robertson, and the prolific Hearts striker eventually spent a short time as a United forward. Moncur stayed at the helm with the Edinburgh club until June 1981 and saw them gain promotion but then slip to relegation at the first time of asking. He was not out of football for long, however, as he moved swiftly to join Devon-based Plymouth Argyle, who were at the time in the old Third Division.

He returned to the North East from Devon in September 1983 and briefly coached non-League Whitley Bay and managed Hartlepool for one year from November 1988 before leaving to concentrate on business issues.

Moncur became a useful sailor in his spare time and shifted up a gear when he retired, competing in several arduous races. He also owned a share in a catamaran that was moored in the Caribbean, sailed several times across the Atlantic Ocean and taught sailing on his beloved Tyne.

A shrewd observer of the game, he enjoyed a good relationship with the media and was a much sought-after radio pundit as well as an entertaining host in the hospitality suites of a revamped St James' Park. Revered in the North East, he was made an honorary freeman of Gateshead in January 2009 as he bravely fought and overcame cancer.

Season	**Appearances**	**Goals**
1962–63	3	0
1963–64	3	0
1964–65	12	0
1965–66	20 (3)	0
1966–67	25	0
1967–68	36	0
1968–69	43	3
1969–70	50	0
1970–71	48	3
1971–72	22	0
1972–73	42	1
1973–74	52	3
Total	**356 (3)**	**10**

BRYAN 'POP' ROBSON

Born: Sunderland, 11 November 1945.

Career as a player: NEWCASTLE UNITED, West Ham United, Sunderland, West Ham United, Sunderland, Carlisle United, Chelsea, Carlisle United (on loan), Sunderland, Carlisle United.

Although Bryan Stanley Robson did not score in either the semi-final or the Final matches of the Fairs Cup, he netted in every other round and with six goals he was the club's top scorer in the competition. Born in Sunderland in 1945, Robson was in his early 20s when Newcastle

landed the Fairs Cup. He was already a proflic goalscorer, despite being only 5ft 8in tall, and from scoring on his debut against Charlton in September 1964 he gave the club sterling service until he departed in February 1971.

By 1965 United were clambering out of the Second Division and slowly but surely Robson was establishing himself as a nippy, energetic forward with an instinctive knack around goal. By the start of the decisive 1968–69 season he was becoming indispensible and his role in the Fairs Cup triumph is difficult to over-emphasize.

Robson was a striker who looked beyond football to improve his all-round game. At one point he trained with ballroom dancer Len Heppell and was thus able to build upon the sprightly movements he had mastered as a county table-tennis player. On the eve of the 1968–69 campaign Robson was training on his own, as well as with Newcastle, running and trying new exercises to increase his flexibility, and that dedication and hard work paid off on the European stage. It is worth noting that he also ended up marrying Len's daughter and even had to cancel the wedding on 11 June and move it to 4 June as United progressed to the two-leg Final.

Of his Fairs Cup goals one stands out above them all. It was his strike against Sporting Lisbon that sent St James' into a frenzy and was reckoned by some who saw it to be the finest-ever United goal. From a Tommy Gibb floated free-kick Wyn Davies nodded the ball towards

Robson. Most players would have waited for the ball to drop, but Robson – fuelled by his dancing exploits perhaps – jumped into the air and volleyed the ball into the roof of the net with stunning force. There are those who swear they saw fans behind the goal instinctively flinch as the ball flew netwards – had it gone past the post or over the bar it would have done serious harm.

Bryan was always reluctant to over-exaggerate the tactical know-how of the Fairs Cup-winning team. Of his strike partnership with Davies he simply said: 'It was all pretty simple stuff really. European defences struggled to handle such an out-and-out physical player as Wyn. And with his phenomenal ability in the air he won so many of the balls he contested that I had rich pickings playing off him.'

In September 1970 United travelled to London and beat West Ham United 2–0. Significantly, Robson scored both goals and in doing so ran Bobby Moore, Billy Bonds and Frank Lampard ragged. Clearly West Ham manager Ron Greenwood made a mental note of Robson's prowess. When Robson added goals against Arsenal and Tottenham, Greenwood made his move and the goal 'Pop' netted against Spurs on 20 February 1971 was his last for United. An England Under-23 international, and with four goals short of a century scored for Newcastle, Bryan Robson was rather surprisingly allowed to become West Ham United's record buy at £145,000. The Irons were rewarded almost instantly when Robson scored on his debut against Nottingham Forest.

In 1973 he was voted West Ham's Player of the Year and all seemed rosy in the East End of London. But was he a North East boy at heart? It certainly looked that way in the summer of 1974. When Sunderland were looking for a striker in July of that year they persuaded West Ham to sell Robson for the same £145,000 fee as the Hammers had paid Newcastle. It was an astonishing twist of fate that saw Robson make his Sunderland debut against none other than Newcastle! He did not score in the Texaco Cup match but showed enough composure and drive to suggest that Sunderland had invested wisely.

Pipped for promotion in that first season back in the North East, Robson had better luck in the next campaign as Sunderland won the Second Division and he finished as the Rokerites' top scorer (he also had the audacity to net against Newcastle in an Anglo-Scottish Cup tie). In October 1976, just months after helping Sunderland win the Second Division, Robson was back in the East End of London and with West Ham United once more. John Lyall was the Hammers boss and Robson made his second West Ham debut against Ipswich Town on 16 October 1976. That second spell in the East End of London allowed Robson to take his scoring tally as a West Ham player to 104, and from only 254 games that was a significant total.

Remarkably, in June 1979 he was sold back to Sunderland, this time for £45,000 in what was becoming a near regular swap! In May 1980 he once again helped the Red and Whites achieve promotion, this time as Second Division runners-up, and with 20 goals for the season he was the club's top marksman. He had scored against United once more, this time in the epic League Cup tie that went Sunderland's way in a 7–6 penalty shoot-out. Robson was by now reaping the benefits of his early dedication and when he scored on his last outing for Sunderland at the tail end of the 1983–84 season he was 38 years old.

After his playing days ended, and there was a stint with Carlisle United squeezed in, he was involved in youth coaching at several clubs – most notably Sunderland, Manchester United and Leeds. His captain at Newcastle, Bobby Moncur, has fond recollections of Robson the striker: 'In my opinion he was the most unlucky guy never to be capped by

England. Bryan had a wonderful ability to put the ball in the back of net from a variety of positions. I later played with him at Sunderland and he was still a prolific marksman at Roker.'

Season	Appearances	Goals
1964–65	20	7
1965–66	25	10
1966–67	39	11
1967–68	12 (1)	4
1968–69	59	30
1969–70	52	24
1970–71	36	10
Total	**243 (1)**	**96**

JIM SCOTT

Born: Falkirk, 21 August 1940.

Career as a player: Denny Rovers, Bo'ness United, Hibernian, NEWCASTLE UNITED, Crystal Palace, Falkirk.

Born in Falkirk in 1940, Jim, like many young Scottish footballers, started his career in the junior ranks (a near equivalent to English non–League football) with Bo'ness United. A right-winger, capable of playing at inside-right, he was a talented youngster and joined Hibernian in October 1958.

After nine years in Edinburgh with Hibernian he had significant European experience, having played 12 times for Hibs in competitive ties. Among his memorable matches were a triumph over two legs against the mighty Barcelona and a compelling clash with Valencia.

In August 1967 Joe Harvey paid Hibs £40,000 and the lively forward set out to emulate his brother Alex, who had won several honours with both

Rangers and Everton. In coming to Newcastle within a year of John McNamee, Jim was helping establish a strong link between the Edinburgh club and Tyneside.

Scott was a most capable goalscorer and had the distinction of scoring Newcastle United's first-ever goal in Europe. Indeed, he took to European football with some style and scored against Feyenoord, Sporting Lisbon, Rangers and Újpest Dozsa; even in the following year's competition he netted against Porto (his last goal for United). Crucially, when he scored against Rangers his goal broke the Glaswegians' resistance.

In February 1970 he was sold to Crystal Palace for £20,000 but by January 1972 he was heading back to his home town of Falkirk, and he ended his senior career at Hamilton Accies, whom he joined in the summer of 1973. However, on 16 February 1974 he broke his leg at Montrose and never played again (by coincidence he had played in 21 games that season as number eight and only switched to number 10 on that fateful day in Angus).

After football Jim stayed in Scotland and at one stage he ran a pub in his native Falkirk.

Season	**Appearances**	**Goals**
1967–68	15 (3)	2
1968–69	39 (2)	7
1969–70	15 (3)	3
Total	**69 (8)**	**12**

JACKIE SINCLAIR

Born: Culross, 21 July 1943.

Career as a player: Dunfermline Athletic, Leicester City, NEWCASTLE UNITED, Sheffield Wednesday, Chesterfield (on loan), Durban City, Dunfermline Athletic, Stenhousemuir.

A left-winger, John 'Jackie' Sinclair came from an impressive footballing background. His brother played with Falkirk and Huddersfield and his uncle, Tommy Wright, was a Sunderland player in the 1950s. Jackie started his senior career during 1960 with Dunfermline Athletic in Fife. He played in the 1965 Scottish Cup Final and was a star pupil in Jock Stein's early 1960s team at Dunfermline; his haul of 34 goals in 61 League appearances was proof enough of this. Crucially, he was experienced on the European stage with Dunfermline and made seven appearances in the Fairs Cup, and this background was very beneficial to Newcastle in later years.

He first sampled England with Leicester City in the summer of 1965 when he was the subject of a £25,000 transfer. His impact in the East Midlands was significant; indeed, he signalled his prowess by scoring on his debut against Liverpool. In the two seasons he spent at Filbert Street he topped the Foxes' scoring charts and netted 50 goals in 103 matches. Jackie also made his only senior Scotland appearance while at Leicester, turning out for the Scots against Portugal at Hampden Park in June 1966. Scotland lost that game and the number seven was a man whom Jackie would eventually team up with at St James' Park – Jim Scott.

It cost Joe Harvey £70,000 to bring Sinclair to Newcastle in January 1968. The 5ft 7in winger was very light, just over 10st, when he joined United and at times he struggled to win over a critical Gallowgate support. Among his early goals was a wonderful strike in the memorable match with Manchester City at St James' when City won 4–3 and in so doing lifted the League Championship. Sinclair was something of an asset in big games and he made his mark in the Fairs Cup by scoring the second goal against Rangers in the crucial semi-final second leg on Tyneside.

Bobby Moncur said of Jackie: 'Jackie provided us with great work rate. That's a theme I repeat with so many of my teammates from this era and quite simply we were a solid team. Jackie had pace and caused a lot of bother for teams out on the left flank. He would track back that bit more than Jimmy on the right flank.'

Sinclair joined Sheffield Wednesday in December 1969 but was unable to help them preserve their First Division status as they slipped into the second tier. Sinclair, like Jim Scott, returned to Scotland, living in Dollar, Clackmannanshire, and working firstly at Stirling University and then as a golf club steward in Fife.

Season	**Appearances**	**Goals**
1967–68	17	3
1968–69	26 (4)	5
1969–70	6	0
Total	**49 (4)**	**8**

GRAHAM WINSTANLEY

Born: Croxdale, 20 January 1948.

Career as a player: NEWCASTLE UNITED, Carlisle United, Brighton, Carlisle United.

Born in Croxdale in 1948, Graham was a United apprentice who was thrust into Inter-Cities Fairs Cup action during an injury crisis. Given that he only played seven League matches in total for the club, his Fairs Cup outing against Sporting Lisbon is an understandable highlight.

Graham, nicknamed 'Tot', left United to join Carlisle United in 1969 and made a good fist of his time with the Cumbrians to the extent that he played in nearly 200 matches for them. He helped Carlisle reach the top flight and a notable teammate at Brunton Park was Chris Balderstone, who doubled up as a cricketer in the summer and reached Test standard with England. Graham's travels were somewhat less exotic and they took him to Brighton in 1974, and there he was able to make 64 League appearances before returning to Carlisle in July 1979 to end his career at senior level. He enjoyed a brief stint with Penrith in non-League football before retiring from the game to settle down in Carlisle working with a wholesale electrical company.

Season	Appearances	Goals
1966–67	1	0
1967–68	3	0
1968–69	3 (1)	0
Total	**7 (1)**	**0**

Fairs Cup Database

Newcastle appearances:

McFaul, Iam	12
Clark, Frank	12
Gibb, Tommy	12
Scott, Jim	12
Robson, Bryan	12
Davies, Wyn	12
Burton, Ollie	11
Craig, David	9
Moncur, Bobby	9
Foggon, Alan	6
Sinclar, Jackie	4
Craggs, John	3
Elliott, David	3
McNamee, John	3
Dyson, Keith	3
Allen, Geoff	2
Horsfield, Arthur	1
Winstanley, Graham	1

(Substitute Appearances)

Sinclair, Jackie	2
Foggon, Alan	2
Iley, Jim	1
Dyson, Keith	1
Bennett, Albert	1
McNamee, John	1
Guthrie, Ron	1

Newcastle goalscorers (24 goals):

Bryan Robson	6
Jim Scott	4
Wyn Davies	4
Tommy Gibb	3
Bobby Moncur	3
Alan Foggon	2
Jackie Sinclair	1
Preben Arentoft	1

Attendances at St James' Park:

Feyenoord	46,348
Sporting Lisbon	53,747
Real Zaragoza	56,055
Vitória Setúbal	57,662
Glasgow Rangers	59,303
Újpest Dozsa	59,234
Total	**332,349**
Average	***55,391***

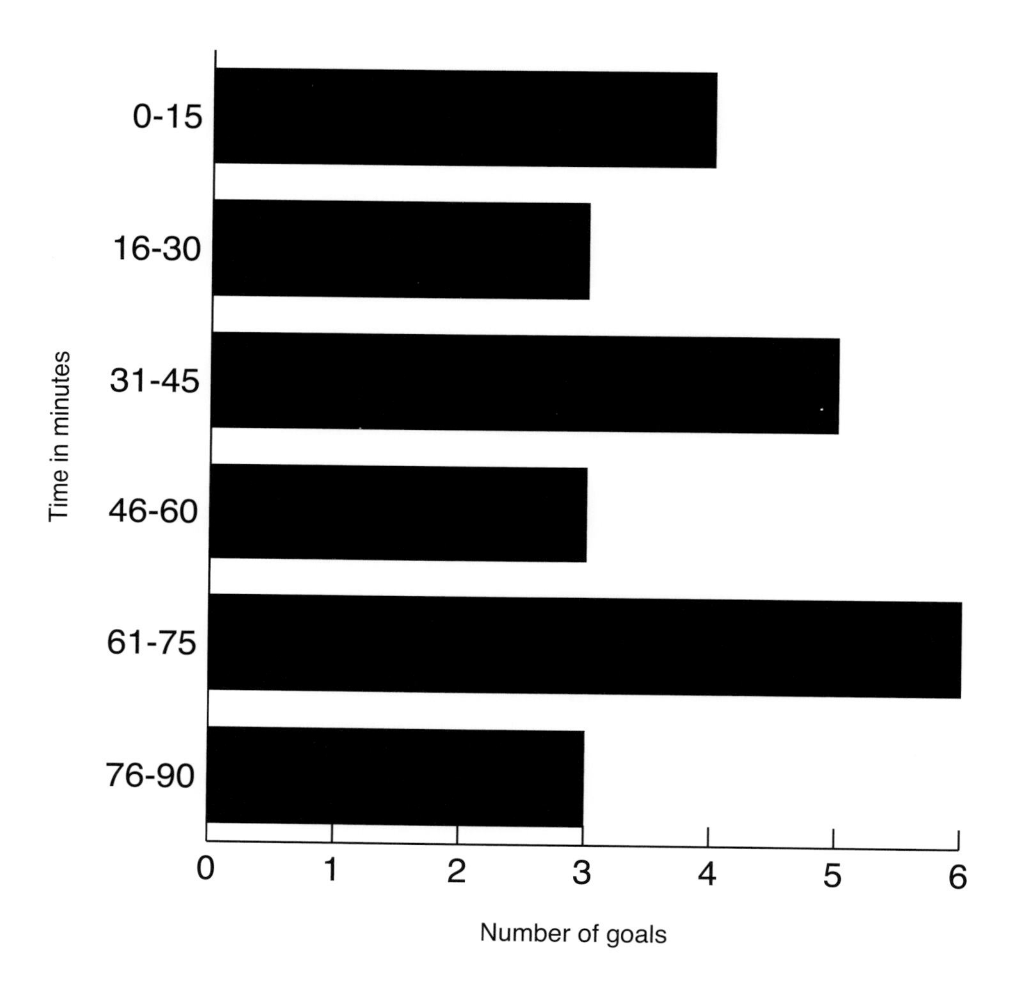
When Newcastle scored
Time in minutes
0-15
16-30
31-45
46-60
61-75
76-90
0
1
2
3
4
5
6
Number of goals

United's Progress at a Glance

1968–69 Inter-Cities Fairs Cup

First Round

First Leg

Newcastle United 4 Feyenoord 0

(Scott, Robson, Gibb, Davies)

Attendance: 46,348

Second Leg

Feyenoord 2 Newcastle United 0

Attendance: 45,000

Second Round

First Leg

Sporting Lisbon 1 Newcastle United 1

(Scott)

Attendance: 9,000

Second Leg

Newcastle United 1 Sporting Lisbon 0

(Robson)

Attendance: 53,747

Third Round

First Leg

Real Zaragoza 3 Newcastle United 2

(Davies, Robson)

Attendance: 22,000

Second Leg

Newcastle United 2 Real Zaragoza 1

(Gibb, Robson)

Attendance: 56,055

Fourth Round

First Leg

Newcastle United 5 Vitória Setúbal 1

(Davies, Foggon, Gibb, Robson 2)

Attendance: 57,662

Second Leg

Vitória Setúbal 3 Newcastle United 1

(Davies)

Attendance: 34,000

Semi-Final

First Leg

Glasgow Rangers 0 Newcastle United 0

Attendance: 75,580

Second Leg

Newcastle United 2 Glasgow Rangers 0

(Scott, Sinclair)

Attendance: 59,303

Final

First Leg

Newcastle United 3 Újpest Dozsa 0

(Moncur 2, Scott)

Attendance: 59,234

Second Leg

Újpest Dozsa 2 Newcastle United 3

(Moncur, Arentoft, Foggon)

Attendance: 34,000

The 1968–69 Season in Detail

(home matches in bold):

RESULTS

August 1968

10	**D1**	**West Ham United**	**D 1–1**	**36,830**
14	D1	Sheffield Wednesday	D 1–1	27,258
17	D1	Burnley	L 0–1	13,500
21	**D1**	**Chelsea**	**W 3–2**	**39,048**
24	**D1**	**Everton**	**D 0–0**	**38,851**
28	**D1**	**Nottingham Forest**	**D 1–1**	**34,613**
31	D1	Sunderland	D 1–1	49,807

September 1968

02	LC	Southport	W 2–0	8,521
07	D1	Coventry City	L 1–2	34,361
11	**Fairs Cup**	**Feyenoord**	**W 4–0**	**46,348**
14	**D1**	**West Bromwich Albion**	**L 2–3**	**35,128**
17	Fairs Cup	Feyenoord	L 0–2	45,000
21	D1	Manchester United	L 1–3	47,262
25	LC	Southampton	L 1–4	13,840
28	**D1**	**Tottenham Hotspur**	**D 2–2**	**30,469**

October 1968

05	**D1**	**Leeds United**	**L 0–1**	**41,999**
08	D1	Nottingham Forest	W 4–2	17,651
12	D1	Ipswich Town	W 4–1	20,763
19	**D1**	**Queens Park Rangers**	**W 3–2**	**35,503**
26	D1	Liverpool	L 1–2	45,323
30	Fairs Cup	Sporting Lisbon	D 1–1	9,000

November 1968

02	**D1**	**Leicester City**	**D 0–0**	**20,374**
09	D1	Arsenal	D 0–0	34,168
16	**D1**	**Manchester City**	**W 1–0**	**36,420**
20	**Fairs Cup**	**Sporting Lisbon**	**W 1–0**	**53,747**
23	D1	Wolverhampton Wanderers	L 0–5	25,425
30	**D1**	**Southampton**	**W 4–1**	**29,515**

December 1968

07	D1	Stoke City	L 0–1	11,594
14	**D1**	**Ipswich Town**	**W 2–1**	**26,454**
21	D1	Queens Park Rangers	D 1–1	16,444
26	D1	Leeds United	L 1–2	44,995

January 1969

01	Fairs Cup	Real Zaragoza	L 2–3	22,000
04	**FAC**	**Reading**	**W 4–0**	**41,255**
11	D1	Leicester City	L 1–2	21,673
15	**Fairs Cup**	**Real Zaragoza**	**W 2–1**	**56,055**
18	**D1**	**Arsenal**	**W 2–1**	**34,227**
25	**FAC**	**Manchester City**	**D 0–0**	**57,994**
29	FAC	Manchester City	L 0–2	60,844

February 1969

15	D1	Southampton	D 0–0	22,213

March 1969

01	D1	West Ham United	L 1–3	26,336
08	**D1**	**Burnley**	**W 1–0**	**32,460**
12	**Fairs Cup**	**Vitória Setúbal**	**W 5–1**	**57,662**
22	**D1**	**Sunderland**	**D 1–1**	**48,588**
26	Fairs Cup	Vitória Setúbal	L 1–3	34,000
29	**D1**	**Coventry City**	**W 2–0**	**26,750**

April 1969

02	D1	Tottenham Hotspur	W 1–0	22,528
04	D1	Chelsea	D 1–1	42,078
09	**D1**	**Sheffield Wednesday**	**W 3–2**	**25,973**
12	**D1**	**Manchester United**	**W 2–0**	**46,379**
14	D1	Everton	D 1–1	36,335
19	D1	West Bromwich Albion	L 1–5	23,087
21	**D1**	**Wolverhampton Wanderers**	**W 4–1**	**24,986**
30	**D1**	**Stoke City**	**W 5–0**	**28,015**

May 1969

05	D1	Manchester City	L 0–1	20,108
14	Fairs Cup	Rangers	D 0–0	75,580
17	**D1**	**Liverpool**	**D 1–1**	**34,927**
21	**Fairs Cup**	**Rangers**	**W 2–0**	**59,303**
29	**Fairs Cup**	**Újpest Dozsa**	**W 3–0**	**59,234**

June 1969

11	Fairs Cup	Újpest Dozsa	W 3–2	34,000

Newcastle Month By Month

Month	*P*	*W*	*D*	*L*	*F*	*A*
August 1968	7	1	5	1	7	7
September 1968	8	2	1	5	13	16
October 1968	6	3	1	2	13	9
November 1968	6	3	2	1	6	6
December 1968	4	1	1	2	4	5
January 1969	7	3	1	3	11	9
February 1969	1	0	1	0	0	0
March 1969	6	3	1	2	11	8
April 1969	8	5	2	1	18	10
May 1969	5	2	2	1	6	2
June 1969	1	1	0	0	3	2

Quite clearly Newcastle's season gathered momentum as it rolled on. They won only two games in a busy September but fortunately one of them was the 4–0 triumph over Feyenoord, which was just sufficient to send them through. Remarkably United's best month was April, yet they did not play a single Inter-Cities Fairs Cup tie in that month. But by losing only three matches in their final 14 of the season they hit form at just the right time.

Season Database

Player	*Total*	*League*	*FA Cup*	*L Cup*	*Other*
Robson, B.	59	42	3	2	12
McFaul, W.	58	41	3	2	12
Gibb, T.	58	41	3	2	12
Clark, F.	54	38	3	1	12
Davies, R.	52	37	3	–	12
Burton, A.	49	33	3	2	11
Moncur, R.	43	30	3	–	10
Scott, J.	39	22	3	2	12
Craig, D.	38	26	1	2	9
Foggon, A.	28	19	3	–	6
McNamee, J.	27	23	–	1	3
Sinclair, J.	26	21	–	1	4
Dyson, K.	21	15	3	–	3
Craggs, J.	20	15	2	–	3
Elliott, D.	19	14	–	2	3
Arentoft, P.	14	10	–	–	4
Allen, G.	13	10	–	1	2
Horsfield, A.	8	7	–	–	1
Guthrie, R.	6	5	–	1	–
Winstanley, G.	3	2	–	–	1
Bennett, A.	3	3	–	–	–
Robson, T.	3	2	–	1	–
Hindson, G.	2	2	–	–	–
Iley, J.	2	1	–	1	–
Ross, W.	2	1	–	1	–
Hope, J.	1	1	–	–	–
Duffy, A.	1	1	–	–	

Goalscorers	*Total*	*League*	*FA Cup*	*L Cup*	*Other*
Robson, B.	30	21	1	2	6
Davies, R.	15	11	–	–	4
Foggon, A.	7	5	–	–	2
Scott, J.	7	2	1	–	4
Gibb, T.	6	4	–	–	2
Dyson, K.	6	5	1	–	–
Sinclair, J.	5	3	–	1	1
Horsfield, A.	3	3	–	–	–
McNamee, J.	3	3	–	–	–
Arentoft, P.	3	2	–	–	1
Moncur, R.	3	–	–	–	3
Allen, G.	1	1	–	–	–
Craig, D.	1	–	1	–	–
Burton, A.	1	1	–	–	–
Own-goals	1	–	–	–	1

1968–69 – Division One final table

	P	*W*	*D*	*L*	*F*	*A*	*Pts*
Leeds U.	42	27	13	2	66	26	67
Liverpool	42	25	11	6	63	24	61
Everton	42	21	15	6	77	36	57
Arsenal	42	22	12	8	56	27	56
Chelsea	42	20	10	12	73	53	50
Tottenham H.	42	14	17	11	61	51	45
Southampton	42	16	13	13	57	48	45
West Ham U.	42	13	18	11	66	50	44
Newcastle U.	**42**	**15**	**14**	**13**	**61**	**55**	**44**
W.B.A.	42	16	11	15	64	67	43
Manchester U.	42	15	12	15	57	53	42
Ipswich T.	42	15	11	16	59	60	41
Manchester C.	42	15	10	17	64	55	40
Burnley	42	15	9	18	55	82	39
Sheffield W.	42	10	16	16	41	54	36
Wolves	42	10	15	17	41	58	35
Sunderland	42	11	12	19	43	67	34
Nottingham F.	42	10	13	19	45	57	33
Stoke C.	42	9	15	18	40	63	33
Coventry C.	42	10	11	21	46	64	31
Leicester C.	42	9	12	21	39	68	30
Q.P.R.	42	4	10	28	39	95	18

1967–68 – Division One final table

		Home					Away					**Totals**						
	Plyd	W	D	L	F	A	*W*	*D*	*L*	*F*	*A*	**W**	**D**	**L**	**F**	**A**	**GD**	Pts
1 Manchester C.	42	17	2	2	52	16	*9*	*4*	*8*	*34*	*27*	**26**	**6**	**10**	**86**	**43**	**+43**	58
2 Manchester U.	42	15	2	4	49	21	*9*	*6*	*6*	*40*	*34*	**24**	**8**	**10**	**89**	**55**	**+34**	56
3 Liverpool	42	17	2	2	51	17	*5*	*9*	*7*	*20*	*23*	**22**	**11**	**9**	**71**	**40**	**+31**	55
4 Leeds U.	42	17	3	1	49	14	*5*	*6*	*10*	*22*	*27*	**22**	**9**	**11**	**71**	**41**	**+30**	53
5 Everton	42	18	1	2	43	13	*5*	*5*	*11*	*24*	*27*	**23**	**6**	**13**	**67**	**40**	**+27**	52
6 Chelsea	42	11	7	3	34	25	*7*	*5*	*9*	*28*	*43*	**18**	**12**	**12**	**62**	**68**	**–6**	48
7 Tottenham H.	42	11	7	3	44	20	*8*	*2*	*11*	*26*	*39*	**19**	**9**	**14**	**70**	**59**	**+11**	47
8 W B A	42	12	4	5	45	25	*5*	*8*	*8*	*30*	*37*	**17**	**12**	**13**	**75**	**62**	**+13**	46
9 Arsenal	42	12	6	3	37	23	*5*	*4*	*12*	*23*	*33*	**17**	**10**	**15**	**60**	**56**	**+4**	44
10 Newcastle U.	**42**	**12**	**7**	**2**	**38**	**20**	***1***	***8***	***12***	***16***	***47***	**13**	**15**	**14**	**54**	**67**	**–13**	**41**
11 Nottingham F.	42	11	6	4	34	22	*3*	*5*	*13*	*18*	*42*	**14**	**11**	**17**	**52**	**64**	**–12**	39
12 W.H.U.	42	8	5	8	43	30	*6*	*5*	*10*	*30*	*39*	**14**	**10**	**18**	**73**	**69**	**+4**	38
13 Leicester C.	42	7	7	7	37	34	*6*	*5*	*10*	*27*	*35*	**13**	**12**	**17**	**64**	**69**	**–5**	38
14 Burnley	42	12	7	2	38	16	*2*	*3*	*16*	*26*	*55*	**14**	**10**	**18**	**64**	**71**	**–7**	38
15 Sunderland	42	8	7	6	28	28	*5*	*4*	*12*	*23*	*33*	**13**	**11**	**18**	**51**	**61**	**–10**	37
16 Southampton	42	9	8	4	37	31	*4*	*3*	*14*	*29*	*52*	**13**	**11**	**18**	**66**	**83**	**–17**	37
17 Wolves	42	10	4	7	45	36	*4*	*4*	*13*	*21*	*39*	**14**	**8**	**20**	**66**	**75**	**–9**	36
18 Stoke City	42	10	3	8	30	29	*4*	*4*	*13*	*20*	*44*	**14**	**7**	**21**	**50**	**73**	**–23**	35
19 Sheffield W.	42	6	10	5	32	24	*5*	*2*	*14*	*19*	*39*	**11**	**12**	**19**	**51**	**63**	**–12**	34
20 Coventry C.	42	8	5	8	32	32	*1*	*10*	*10*	*19*	*39*	**9**	**15**	**18**	**51**	**71**	**–20**	33
21 Sheffield U.	42	7	4	10	25	31	*4*	*6*	*11*	*24*	*39*	**11**	**10**	**21**	**49**	**70**	**–21**	32
22 Fulham	42	6	4	11	27	41	*4*	*3*	*14*	*29*	*57*	**10**	**7**	**25**	**56**	**98**	**–42**	27

References and further reading

Books

Rothmans Football Yearbook – Football Annual, published by Headline

World Football Handbooks – Compiled by Brian Glanville

Football League – Players Record 1946–1992 – Editor B. Hugman

Newspapers

The Newcastle Chronicle

The Times

The Dundee Courier

The Guardian

The Scotsman

The Glasgow Herald

Programmes:

Newcastle United home programmes from Cup run.

England programmes various 1964–1970.

Web sites

www.toonarama.co.uk

A lovingly crafted website that contains a detailed and occasionally humorous section on the Inter-Cities Fairs Cup run.

www.khscott.org.uk/nufc/

A detailed website that gives chapter and verse on every player who represented Newcastle United since 1946. Crammed with statistics this is a real treasure trove of Newcastle history.